CONTINUOUSLY
COMMUNICATE!

People-Centric Skills

The Wiley Corporate F&A series provides information, tools, and insights to corporate professionals responsible for issues affecting the profitability of their company, from accounting and finance to internal controls and performance management.

Founded in 1807, John Wiley & Sons is the oldest independent publishing company in the United States. With offices in North America, Europe, Asia, and Australia, Wiley is globally committed to developing and marketing print and electronic products and services for our customers' professional and personal knowledge and understanding.

People-Centric Skills

*Interpersonal and Communication
Skills for Auditors and
Business Professionals*

DANNY M. GOLDBERG

MANNY ROSENFELD

Published by John Wiley & Sons, Inc., Hoboken, New Jersey.
Published simultaneously in Canada.

For general information on our other products and services or for technical support, please contact our Customer Care Department within the United States at (800) 762-2974, outside the United States at (317) 572-3993 or fax (317) 572-4002.

Wiley publishes in a variety of print and electronic formats and by print-on-demand. Some material included with standard print versions of this book may not be included in e-books or in print-on-demand. If this book refers to media such as a CD or DVD that is not included in the version you purchased, you may download this material at http:// booksupport.wiley.com. For more information about Wiley products, visit www.wiley.com.

Library of Congress Cataloging-in-Publication Data:

ISBN 978-1-118-85081-7 (Hardcover)
ISBN 978-1-118-92536-2 (ePDF)
ISBN 978-1-118-92537-9 (ePub)

Printed in the United States of America
10 9 8 7 6 5 4 3 2 1

Danny: To my wife, Kate, and my wonderful kids, Caleb and Liora, who inspire me on a daily basis.

Manny: To Louise, my wonderful, loving, and supportive wife of 32 years. She has gracefully and patiently managed being married to an auditor and engineer—no easy feat!

Contents

Chapter 1 The People-Centric Journey Begins

People-Centric (P-C) Skills aim to improve all aspects of personal interactions, relationship development, and communications. These skills are as essential to success as are the technical skills. The People-Centric Skills include, but are not limited to: communication in all mediums, conflict resolution, active listening, leadership, mentoring and coaching, establishing business relationships, effective teaming and team dynamics, consensus building, nonverbal communications and body language, assessing corporate culture, etc.

Chapter 2 Agreeing to the Plan

- Generating and prioritizing ideas within a group
- Brainstorming
- Multivoting
- Avoiding Groupthink

Chapter 3 Corporate Culture Mentoring

- Mentoring
- Assessing Corporate Culture

Chapter 4 Managing Conflict with Difficult Executives

- Conflict Management
- Effective Meetings

Foreword

I N 2013, the Institute of Internal Auditors (IIA) and Robert Half released research entitled "7 Attributes of Highly Effective Internal Auditors." Coauthored by the IIA's president and CEO, Richard Chambers, and by Paul McDonald, senior executive director from Robert Half, this piece was a giant leap forward for the profession of internal auditing. This article moved the dialog from the "technician" internal auditor to the consummate "soft skills" internal auditor. Among the seven attributes, they included communication, teamwork, partnering, and relationship building.

As a veteran chief auditor for more than 25 years in the airline business (Eastern, Continental, and United Airlines), I have advocated that while technical skills, including "knowing the business," are important ingredients for a successful internal auditor, it is strong interpersonal skill sets that truly differentiate the world-class internal auditor from the competent one. I have even asserted that given the choice of having the gold medal winner on the CPA or CIA exam on my team or the top soft skills candidate, I would select the top interpersonal skills person every time.

My own background does not follow the traditional accountant/auditor path. My father was an ordained minister whose undergraduate major was English. He instilled in me a love of writing and oratory. In high school, I competed in many essay contests and won a number of them. In college, while my degree was in accounting, I also took numerous English courses as well as a public speaking course.

I believe that our business schools, while preparing future accountants/auditors well for the technical side of their profession, can still optimize their programs by offering more extensive business writing and public speaking courses, and further enhance their curriculums by including more sociology and behavioral sciences sessions. I am pleased that, as I have sat across from Fortune 500 executives and board members, I have had the ability and confidence to hold the attention of those leaders both in oral and written communications.

In 2006–2007, I had the honor to serve as the IIA's Global Chairman of the Board. During that period I traveled the globe speaking with internal auditors and I had the privilege of meeting with political and government leaders, including the auditor generals of China, Mexico, and Peru. My theme for that year was "Tell the World." I truly felt that internal auditors had a responsibility to tell the world, both in writing and orally, about what great value we bring to our organizations and stakeholders.

I have been privileged to know both of the authors of this book and recognize their passion and enthusiasm for both the internal audit profession as well as the soft skills training so needed for today's internal auditors. I have seen Danny Goldberg at numerous IIA events leading "state-of-the-art" training sessions, and was so impressed with his passion and quality of training that I use him to provide training for my teams.

I highly recommend this book, *People-Centric Skills*, to the internal audit and business community. It is one of the few books written by internal audit professionals themselves about ways to improve our own skills to be better team players in our departments; to assist us in resolving conflicts both within our teams as well as with those we are tasked with auditing; and to help us become the most effective internal auditors we can be. I would suggest this book should be a mandatory read for all internal auditors, just like reading the *International Professional Practices Framework (IPPF)* or *Sawyer's Guide for Internal Auditors*.

Steve Goepfert, CIA, CPA, CRMA
Retired Vice President Internal Audit
United Airlines

Preface

PEOPLE-CENTRIC SKILLS: *Interpersonal and Communication Skills for Auditors and Business Professionals* is a comprehensive guide to the "soft skills" that make technical professionals more effective. People-Centric Skills aim to improve all aspects of professional interactions, relationship development, and communication. These skills are as essential to success as are technical capabilities. This is the easy-to-read story of a dynamic and leading internal audit department taking that next step to becoming a world-class audit organization in a fictional company. The foundation of that next step is developing their People-Centric Skills. The book demonstrates the impact that interpersonal and communication skills—whether good or bad—have on an auditor's effectiveness, job, and career. Readers will be able to empathize with the characters, and relate to the real-life situations in which they find themselves. Each chapter features a summary of key People-Centric points and guidelines that will help readers apply what they've learned to their own projects and departments. While the story centers on an internal audit team, the concepts and lessons are broadly applicable to any professional whose success requires the ability to work effectively with others.

In a landmark 2013 study sponsored by the Institute of Internal Auditors (IIA), the seven key attribute areas identified to be a successful auditor include relationship building, partnering, communications, teamwork, diversity, continuous learning, and integrity. Unfortunately, most professionals never obtain these skills as part of their college degrees, certifications, and other ongoing training. They are left to their own varying experiences when it comes to developing these talents. Many career-limiting interactions are likely to occur while these skills remain unrefined. *People-Centric Skills: Interpersonal and Communication Skills for Auditors and Business Professionals* focuses on many of these critical attributes.

Topics include:

- Conflict Management
- Active Listening

- Nonverbal Communications
- Assessing Corporate Culture
- Coaching and Mentoring
- Building an Effective Team and Team Dynamics
- Team Leadership
- Partnering and Relationship Building
- Effective Meeting Practices
- Brainstorming and Multivoting
- Consensus Building

These skills transfer across a broad range of business professions and industries, and from professional to personal life. They open doors, establish effective relationships, improve effectiveness, and can turn a "no" into a "yes." They are the true differentiators in advancing a career. For an auditor, or other professional, to be truly effective, great interpersonal skills are some of the most important tools in the toolbox. This book is a straightforward guide to getting along, getting what you want in a constructive manner, and becoming a world-class professional.

CHAPTER 1: THE PEOPLE-CENTRIC JOURNEY BEGINS

This first chapter introduces the readers to our main characters, Dalton Zimmer, professional speaker and trainer, and Matt Sanders, chief audit executive for MultiCrown Corporation. The chapter focuses on establishing the relationship between Dalton and Matt, and MultiCrown's engagement of Dalton to assist the internal audit team in developing their People-Centric skills.

CHAPTER 2: AGREEING TO THE PLAN

Chapter 2 concerns MultiCrown's annual risk assessment. The audit leadership team gathers to identify the initial key risks of the organization in order to develop the audit plan for the coming year. The chapter centers on the interactions between team members, both positive and negative, as they work to nondefensively generate ideas and subsequently hone in on the critical few. At the same time, they strive to avoid the trap of falsely seeming to agree with each other just to avoid conflict, while secretly harboring reservations.

CHAPTER 3: CORPORATE CULTURE MENTORING

This chapter centers on Matt establishing a mentoring relationship with his audit director, Meghan Dorsch. This type of relationship enables Matt to provide advanced People-Centric advice to Meghan. This initial mentoring discussion focuses on how to read corporate cultures and subcultures, and how to successfully adapt to the unspoken expectations of an organization.

CHAPTER 4: MANAGING CONFLICT WITH DIFFICULT EXECUTIVES

Chapter 4 addresses the initial reason that Dalton was asked by Matt to assist MultiCrown: conflict resolution. Matt and Dalton help Bill Dorset, an audit manager, in resolving a conflict with one of their very difficult audit clients, Tom Peterson, the president of a large division. This chapter takes readers through the conflict resolution process in order to progress to more positive and mutually beneficial interactions.

CHAPTER 5: COACHING A LEADER TO FORM A TEAM

This chapter concentrates on two main themes: Team roles and coaching. Matt commissions a special-purpose team to assist the Repair and Maintenance (R&M) organization by developing an audit program focusing on improving the effectiveness of the R&M processes. The chapter explores the challenges of coaching a leader to launch a cross-functional team of R&M engineers and auditors to accomplish this task. This includes delving into the roles of the team leader, team members, facilitator, and sponsor. Additionally, the chapter covers the Situational Leadership model and how to apply it in an organization.

CHAPTER 6: TEAM DYNAMICS: SETTING THE FOUNDATION FOR SUCCESS

Chapter 6 continues to discuss the progress of the R&M audit team and the development of an operational audit discipline. The team goes through the stages of team development: *forming, norming, storming,* and *performing*. It also discusses the importance of Team Ground Rules and the Team Mission

Statement in the development of an effective team. Finally, in the performing stage, the team focuses on building consensus and working together as an effective team.

CHAPTER 7: COMMUNICATING TO BUILD RELATIONSHIPS

This chapter continues to discuss and develop the importance of interpersonal skills. In this chapter, Dalton assists the audit team in developing a communication and promotion plan to effectively explain audit's objectives to the organization. This issue arises as a new executive joins MultiCrown and Matt wants to begin their relationship in a positive and constructive manner. Significant aspects of relationship building include transparency and constant communication, optimized and active listening, and the ability to read body language and gesture clusters.

CHAPTER 8: CONTINUING THE PEOPLE-CENTRIC JOURNEY

The final chapter takes our main characters to the year-end week of training. It focuses on finalizing and summarizing what has occurred during the year and reviewing the key People-Centric lessons for all team members. It also begins to establish possible future paths to continue the People-Centric journey for this engaging, ascending, and hard-driving team, and their now-beloved consultant.

WHAT IS YOUR STORY?

The objective of this book is to share practical knowledge on interpersonal and communication skills with the world of auditors and other business professionals. To communicate this knowledge, we follow characters Dalton Zimmer, executive trainer and coach, and Matt Sanders, chief audit executive of the fictional MultiCrown Corporation, through myriad situations. Dalton assists the audit team in not only handling these difficult situations, but also teaching them to prospectively manage these interactions in the future.

Acknowledgments

WE PARTICULARLY THANK Louise Rosenfeld for her many long hours of review and invaluable editorial assistance on this book. Not only did she help us smooth the dialog into a more natural form, she also helped us keep the characters true to themselves.

People-Centric Skills

CHAPTER ONE

The People-Centric Journey Begins

People-Centric Skills

People-Centric (P-C) Skills aim to improve all aspects of personal interactions, relationship development, and communications. These skills are as essential to success as are the technical skills. The People-Centric Skills include, but are not limited to: communication in all mediums, conflict resolution, active listening, leadership, mentoring and coaching, establishing business relationships, effective teaming and team dynamics, consensus building, nonverbal communications and body language, assessing corporate culture, etc.

MATT SANDERS STOOD with his hands behind his back, pensively looking out the 12-story window of his office building. It was a bright, sunny, and crisp autumn day in Chicago. His view of the Chicago River, and the hypnotic procession of boats, helped calm his uncharacteristically frayed nerves.

Matt glanced at his reflection in the floor-to-ceiling window of his office. In the reflection, he saw a 47-year-old executive intently staring back. He is six feet tall, but like most men, usually thought of himself as a couple of inches taller; he has a square firm jaw, prominent nose, piercing dark eyes, and an erect military bearing from his tour with the Air Force. His dark hair has streaks of gray at the temples, which he has reluctantly convinced himself makes him look more distinguished. At least Leslie, his wife, tells him so. His audit staff see him as an intelligent, warm, even-tempered, and caring leader with a very dry, self-deprecating sense of humor. With wry amusement, he thought that in all humbleness, he had to agree with them.

As the head of Internal Audit for MultiCrown Corporation, Matt had a team of 33 auditors currently scattered over four continents. He was proud to be an officer of the Corporation, one of the world's most reputable and admired advanced materials companies. The Company was founded almost 100 years ago, and used to be very paternalistic, stodgy, and resistant to change. However, under the capable leadership of MultiCrown's current CEO, Caleb Line, it has transformed its culture into a modern, progressive organization, with a high degree of technological innovation focused on customers. MultiCrown has, over the past decade, reinvented itself from a basic aluminum, copper, steel, and plastics company into a diversified global manufacturing company that makes and markets advanced material composites. The senior executive team, of which Matt is a member, has been very focused on creating a world-class organization and having a strong and ethical culture. Matt thought it had succeeded in this, with the exception of a few employees. The Corporation has had consistently high profit margins over the past eight years, and operating revenue that recently reached the $15 billion mark, firmly entrenching it as a Fortune 500 corporation. Of its five diverse businesses, three were very profitable, one had turned the corner and was starting to show a modest profit, and one division, the Plastics Molding Division, was rapidly going downhill. They had been consistently losing money for three years.

Matt prided himself on having composed, orderly thoughts, but this morning he was struggling. A couple of his audit teams were having problems, and Bill Dorset, the manager of his audit team in Mobile, Alabama, was experiencing significant difficulties dealing with the prickly and explosive head of the Plastics Molding Division, Tom Peterson. They really seemed to be miscommunicating.

Since the original definition of the word *auditor* is "one who listens," Matt reflected on the irony of his staff's current problems being mostly due to missteps in communications. As he had come to realize over the past few years, auditors and other business professionals, while receiving a heavy dose of training in "hard" technical skills via their college degrees and certifications, were woefully deficient in their interpersonal, communication, and other "soft" skills. Matt was determined to close his team's skills gap.

Matt snapped out of his reverie to note that it was almost 8:00 A.M., and Dalton Zimmer was due to arrive at his office. At just that moment, as Matt turned from the window, his ultra-efficient and elegant executive assistant, Lila Carlson, entered his office. Lila is a statuesque, 35-something, dynamic single woman with auburn-reddish hair reaching to her shoulders. "Mr. Zimmer is here—do you want to see him now?"

"Thank you, Lila, yes, please bring him in," Matt replied with understated anticipation.

Dalton's jovial and expressive face lit up with a smile as he entered Matt's office. He was relaxed, energetic, and confident and sported a shaved head and goatee. Dalton always joked that he had long flowing locks, and shaving his head was just a stylistic choice—but no, it definitely was *not* a choice. Dalton strived to differentiate himself from the currently casual standard corporate look as he always wore a three-piece suit, matching pocket square with tie, and his grandfather's pocket watch neatly tucked into his vest pocket. Dalton has always been known for his boisterous personality and outgoing demeanor, a true product of his vocation. As a professional speaker, trainer, and career coach, Dalton's business was built on his ability to engage people and connect with anyone and everyone. Prior to his current profession, Dalton was the head of audit for a midsized retailer, so Matt felt comfortable that he could relate to his current difficulties.

Matt warmly shook his hand in welcome. "Dalton, great to see you! I want to tell you again how much we appreciated your People-Centric training on interpersonal skills for our auditors last spring. It wet our appetite for a much heavier infusion of your concepts, and, quite frankly, I'm now seeing the need for it more and more."

"I can't thank you enough for bringing me back and I'm excited to be here," Dalton replied. "I have traded emails with your team since my P-C training and I can see that it was very thought-provoking for your staff. What do you have in mind when you say a 'heavier infusion' of training?" Dalton asked eagerly, sensing a business opportunity.

With Matt gesturing to the two wingchairs at the other end of his office, both men settled in comfortably with cups of coffee invisibly provided by Lila. "When you did your training," Matt explained, "you told us that a two-day session was only enough to raise awareness of how critical good communications and soft skills are to the success of an internal audit organization. You *did* warn us that it would not cover the majority of the possible topics in much depth."

Matt, usually careful in what he said, paused for a few seconds to consider his proposal. "Dalton, what we really need now is practical P-C Skills advice *at the point* we're interacting with our audit clients and with each other. That would help our auditors and managers cement these skills via real interactions. Also, selfishly, I hope you can make those interactions go better for us. We've had a few rough ones lately!" Dalton nodded to signal his close attention and to encourage Matt to keep explaining.

Matt continued, "Quite frankly, your class provoked a lot of thoughts and suggestions from the group and we are now ready to retool our communications and interactions. I believe this will help our relationships with our auditees and significantly drive us to be a more effective audit group. Based on what I have seen over the past few months, I do think we need more than just a longer training session; we need hands-on, situational, direct coaching. I'm willing to invest in the future success of my team."

"Dalton, what I'd like to propose is for you to join us for several months as a P-C coach. The audit managers and I can decide which of our audits, exit conferences, planning meetings, risk discussions, and so on could benefit the most from your advice and expertise. I want you to help us prepare for each selected interaction, sit through each, provide guidance, later help us debrief after the event, and finally, give us suggestions for the future. At the end of your coaching period, we could have additional training where you can share the events and related lessons with the entire audit staff."

Dalton tried to hide his excitement and continued to nod thoughtfully as Matt explained what he wanted. "These are great ideas, Matt, but some of your auditors and managers may feel threatened by what they see as possible criticism and someone looking over their shoulder," he cautioned.

Realizing the truth in this, Matt thought for several long moments before he responded: "We'll need to help the staff see that just as we make improvement recommendations to others and expect them not to get defensive, we also must accept suggestions. Otherwise, we're being hypocrites!" Matt then went on, "However, it's a valid caution, and I'll emphasize to the staff that your assistance is meant to be a positive step for us. We have a great group and I am not planning to change the makeup of the team. I'm not looking to blame or criticize anybody. What we all should want is to have a leading-class audit organization."

Dalton said enthusiastically, "Matt, that sounds great; this is a very novel approach to this problem and is a very exciting project to undertake. I'm very interested in helping you and your team! How do you want to proceed?"

"Great!" Matt exclaimed, "How about if you look at your schedule and put together a quote and proposal on timing? Please remember, we have to fit this in our budget, so be kind to us. Once we reach agreement, we could meet with a couple of my managers to jointly lay out some of the upcoming events we want your help with."

"You guys always get my best rate! I can probably carve out 8 to 10 weeks of assistance in the next six months or so, but not continuously. I have other obligations and we'll need to work around them." In his mind, Matt cynically challenged the "best rate" comment; however, Dalton had been fair with them and had delivered good value in the past. While Matt was distracted with his private thoughts, Dalton continued: "How about if I get back to you tomorrow with a proposal?"

On such an upbeat note, both men got up, and Matt shook Dalton's hand as he escorted him to the door. On his way down the elevator, Dalton had to contain his excitement as this was definitely a new and profitable type of project. A renowned speaker and writer, Dalton had undertaken more than a few interesting jobs over the years, but not many audit shops "opened their doors" fully to an Interpersonal Coach. This was a truly unique experience and just about the right timing; with his divorce now settling, being on the road and very busy is just what the doctor prescribed! He also mentally, but enthusiastically, patted himself on the back with both arms for branding the bundle of interpersonal, communications, and other "soft" skills as the much-catchier "People-Centric Skills" concept. As he exited the building, his thoughts strayed to his social media campaign to introduce the *P-C* term. He was ecstatic with how well it was working.

• • •

During the week following his discussion with Dalton, Matt actively sought support from the Audit Committee and the Company's CEO, Caleb Line, to bring Dalton in for the P-C skills project with Internal Audit. With Matt's vast experience and his consistent professionalism leading the audit team, the Audit Committee and Caleb have always had high confidence in his ideas and judgment. In fact, the Audit Committee Chair, Larry Worthem, was very excited about this cutting-edge development program. "If this works out, I have a few more audit committees I serve on that could use this type of training in the organizations." Caleb also agreed, and Matt remembered him stating, "MultiCrown Corporation has been successful for 100 years because we do not rest on our laurels. We are looking to constantly improve." Matt further remembered his kidding smile when he said, "If this People-Centric stuff can really make the auditors popular, it might be something we push through to the entire organization!"

Matt wasn't sure about his auditors being "popular," but with such a ringing endorsement, Matt finalized the agreement and asked Lila to schedule a session with his U.S. audit management team plus Dalton to focus on the highest-priority needs.

• • •

On a cold November morning, Lila escorted Dalton into the audit conference room to meet with the team. Matt's ever-efficient assistant had a glint in her eyes and seemed to have developed a proprietary attitude toward Dalton. Matt looked at the two of them and thought "*hmmm. . . .*" He was not sure what was going on, but hoped Lila would not distract Dalton too much before the project was completed.

Matt, Dalton, and Lila were joined by Meghan Dorsch, MultiCrown's Audit Director; Jim Franklin, IT Audit Director; Linda Hernandez, IT Audit Manager; Bill Dorset, Audit Manager; and Lee Akisodo, Audit Manager.

Matt began by walking the team through an overview of the key objectives for the meeting. "As we have discussed over the past few months, we have some communication and interpersonal areas that we could improve upon. You all know Dalton, and because you and the team thought so highly of his P-C training and suggestions, we are bringing him back to observe our staff in action for a few months, and figure out how we can further improve our P-C skills. This is open to anything and everything in dealing with people. In essence, P-C means putting people at the center, or focusing on human interactions. For example, Dalton is going to work with me in reformulating our Internal Audit 'branding' and communication plan for management. We have had mostly informal and ad-hoc communications, but I want to make sure the Audit Committee and MultiCrown management are fully aware of everything we do to help this company succeed.

"In my opinion, here are some areas we could focus on: establishing positive relations with our stakeholders; improving all facets of communication with them, including planning, risk assessment, and audit exit conferences; improving our own teamwork and developing good team dynamics; and preventing and managing conflict. There are probably many other areas we can focus on. Anyway, these are my initial thoughts, but what I really want is to hear *your* ideas."

Bill was the first to nervously chime in: "Matt, I hope my problems with Tom Peterson are not the reason we are taking this approach; regardless, Dalton's guidance is something we definitely want. I promised Tom a follow-up conversation and I need some good, unbiased insights." Matt spent a few minutes calming Bill's fears and misgivings and allowing the conversation to continue.

Linda was very interested in "nonverbal communication" and thought this could be of significant value to the audit team, especially for her boss, Jim. "Matt, this is awesome! I really like the topic of 'Body Language' and think it can really help us!" As most of the team nodded agreement with Linda, Jim's mouth puckered as if he had sucked on a lemon and his facial expressions were easily read by all, but not commented on. Dalton, a very savvy nonverbal communicator, noted this for future reference.

Meghan added, "I'm not sure if performance appraisals are a hot-button issue, but it's something we struggle with, especially since the management turnover last year. We may want to consider it. I also really agree with your idea to work on the branding of our audit department. Quite frankly, people still hear the word 'auditor' and think of the IRS. Then they might hear 'Certified Public Accountant' and think auditors are all 'numbers' people. I think our organization does not get what internal audit is, or can be. I believe we need to continue to inform our company as to how we can help, and take away the stigma behind audit." A long discussion ensued on this topic, with both Dalton and Matt agreeing that this is an area to focus on.

Jim, usually reluctant to speak in front of a group, saw the pause in the conversation as an opportunity to discuss the issues he had with getting the right information from the Information Technology (IT) department in a timely manner. "I think a great topic would be to understand how we, as auditors, can convince people to do things that they don't necessarily want to do and don't really have to do. For example, pulling requested information, assisting us with questions in a timely manner, and so on." Matt was impressed that Jim had chimed in at all and encouragingly replied: "Jim, great thought! How can we influence people to cooperate without having direct organizational power over them? That's something I am sure many auditors struggle with."

As the morning slowly shifted to the lunch hour, the group began to feel confident that the major areas had been covered.

Dalton, always the considerate gentleman, wanted to get the thoughts of the non-auditor in the room—Lila. Dalton began, "Lila, you have been quiet, but reading your body language and facial expressions, you definitely have something on your mind. Please. . . ." Lila, obviously delighted with this recognition from Dalton, stated, "Well, with the team all over the world, I constantly see the cultural differences that come into play. For example, I know that the last time Dave, a senior auditor on our team, was in Mexico, he told me that he was given advice by José Aguayo, our CFO there. José was kind enough to explain the different cultural approaches and communications styles between the United States and Mexico, to make sure the audit went off well. I'm sure as our auditors travel all over the world, these types of cultural differences get in the way of great communications."

Dalton quickly responded: "I think exploring cultural differences would be a great topic of discussion for the entire team. It is an advanced P-C concept, and it may need to wait until the near the end of our project." Everyone in the room, including the ever-skeptical Jim, was impressed with Lila's suggestion.

Dalton briefly started to mention an amusing personal story to the group about how his lack of cultural understanding almost caused a significant issue with a female CFO. However, a phone call from the chairman of the Audit Committee interrupted the meeting at this time, and when Matt returned to the conference room, Dalton had finished the story, with the group sharing in the rather humorous and embarrassing moment. Rather than have the team hear the story again, Matt suggested they continue their People-Skills deployment plan.

After another hour and with a deeply satisfied breath, Matt said, "I think this has been a very productive meeting. I really appreciate how all of you are jumping into this effort with such enthusiasm. Lila, can you send out your notes to all of us with the topics we've tentatively laid out? Thanks! For the next step, Dalton and I will get together and prioritize the list and begin to work on scheduling. Thanks again, everybody!"

Prior to Dalton leaving, Matt had to ask him about the story with the CFO and the cultural issues. "It sounded like you were going into a priest-and-rabbi joke," Matt said with a smile. Dalton, laughing, dove into the short, but comical learning experience:

"When I worked at BlueSky Beverages, which is, as you know, one of the world's favorite beverages, I spent a good amount of time at our subsidiary in Mexico. I met the CFO, Maria, a very intelligent, and quite frankly, gorgeous woman. In Mexico, prior to really working with each other, you should establish personal relationship and rapport. To that end, when we initially traveled to Mexico City, we spent our first evening there hosted by Maria and her executive team. It was a very nice event, full of good food and drinks. When we called it an evening, tradition would call for a kiss on the cheek as a goodbye. However, I am half French, and the tradition there calls for a kiss on each cheek. Well, Maria kissed me on the cheek, and then I went in for the second kiss on the other side, which in her panicked, startled movement, hit her lips! She jumped back, laughing nervously and saying, "One kiss, one kiss only!" It was very comical and after explaining my background, she understood the situation, but it took me a few years to live it down with her. You cannot make this stuff up! Bottom line is everyone must know their audience and their cultural and social norms."

Matt, shaking his head, exclaimed, "Dalton, this stuff only happens to you." As Matt knows, Dalton frequently ends his implausible stories with the line: "You cannot make this stuff up!" After getting to know Dalton, Matt has come to believe that all of these stories are indeed factual, although he suspects a few embellishments now and then.

Matt walked Dalton to the elevator and commented on the great kickoff meeting. Dalton replied, "I am really pleased with how it went!"

Before pressing the elevator button, Dalton sheepishly asked, "Listen, Matt, since we have known each other for quite a while, I do have a personal question—do you know if Lila is seeing anyone?"

Matt, with his best poker face, remarked, "I don't think Lila is seeing anybody right now, but she is pretty private about her social life. I think she might like you, though."

With that, Dalton smiled and got on the elevator. As the door closed, Dalton laughed and replied, "That's what I read as well. If we have time, we should chat on body language. She was definitely giving off favorable gestures!"

As Matt walked back to his office, he shook his head thinking about Dalton. He was truly a unique and interesting individual. The P-C project was going to be full of surprises.

Matt then switched gears to think about his twenty-third wedding anniversary with Leslie. He was really looking forward to their celebration that night at the new Spanish Tapas restaurant in Lincoln Park. He also hoped she would like the lapis and gold earrings he picked up for her when he was in Brazil the previous month.

Just as Matt was leaving his office for the day, Lila handed him the list that she had prepared during the meeting with Dalton. "I hope you and Leslie have a great anniversary," she brightly said. "Thanks, Lila, we plan on it!" he replied.

Initial People-Centric Topics for Dalton's Involvement

- Team dynamics/forming teams/making teams more effective
- Generating and prioritizing ideas
- Communication and listening skills
- Reaching consensus
- Conflict management/resolution
- Reading body language/nonverbal communications
- Influencing others
- Coaching/mentoring
- Branding Internal Audit
- Establishing constructive relations with key stakeholders
- Assessing the corporate culture
- Effective interactions in a multicultural setting

2

Agreeing to the Plan

People-Centric Skills

Generating and prioritizing ideas within a group; Brainstorming; Multivoting; Avoiding Groupthink

MATT PICKED UP his cell phone and, knowing the quirkiness of its speech recognition program, very carefully enunciated: "Call Dalton's mobile." In a mechanical, but disturbingly feminine voice, his phone acknowledged the command. Matt was relieved, as always, when his phone actually understood him. He chuckled to himself as he remembered getting the toy store, "Doll Town," the last time he asked his smart phone to call "Dalton."

Dalton's ever-cheerful voice came on. "Hi, Matt, what's up, my friend? Are we still on for this morning's session with your team?"

"Hi, Dalton. Yes, we're on, but I'm hoping for a short private discussion before you get here. Do you have a few minutes? There are specific reasons why I wanted you involved in this risk assessment effort, but we haven't had a chance to discuss them in detail."

Dalton replied, "Of course, let's talk; the more I understand the situation, the better I'll be able to help."

Matt continued, "The last time we had a full Audit Leadership Team meeting, with our international managers in town, we had a difficult situation. I'm sure you remember what Meghan is like. She's brilliant, hardworking, dedicated, and focused on doing the best for MultiCrown. I'm very supportive of her and think she has what it takes to potentially grow to be an executive for MultiCrown. However, she's still rough around the edges where people issues are concerned.

"I promoted her to Audit Director when she joined us. She was an audit manager in her last company, but she led only a small team of auditors. She's still getting used to working at a higher managerial level, where she needs to draw out ideas from others and get the best out of a team of over 30 auditors and managers. She is still mostly a doer and struggles with delegation and trust. She likes others to know how smart she is, and in the process, shoots down other people's ideas in a way that is not constructive. Others turn off around her, in my opinion, due to a lack of trust. I think she's a caring person and means well, but maybe she's insecure in her current role. When I made Meghan an Audit Director here, I debated with myself if she had sufficient leadership skills. She was very convincing during the interview.

"Her last company had a much more aggressive corporate culture than we have, and she doesn't quite understand the more collaborative style we like around here. At the last Audit Lead Team meeting, she had good ideas, but was very pushy in how they were presented; the others were intimidated and did not contribute as much as I know they could. I tried pretty hard to counter this and encourage the others, but also didn't want to publicly undermine Meghan. To make matters worse, our international managers are a bit unsure about Meghan's power and influence and they tend to get very quiet around her.

"After that last meeting, I had a long discussion with Meghan, and she seems to be improving. As I said, she's smart, but she still falls back to her old ways sometimes. What I'm hoping to get from you is a structured approach to generating a good list of risks to MultiCrown via the Brainstorming and Multivoting tools. Since there are rules to follow with these tools, I hope that Meghan will go along with the process and learn how to draw out ideas from others in a constructive manner. I especially want our international managers to feel welcomed and encouraged to contribute."

Matt paused to give Dalton a chance to comment. "I've seen this overly aggressive tendency in Meghan from the training I did with your department.

I'll explain the Brainstorming and Multivoting process again, and this will let me coach her when she seems to violate these rules. I'll also work to bring out the quieter members of the team. One of the things I'll also cover is Avoiding Groupthink. When people are afraid of conflict, or afraid of disturbing the peace, they go along with the more aggressive team members, which it sounds like has occurred with Meghan. Additionally, if they believe their ideas will fall on deaf ears, they tend not to even suggest their ideas. This does avoid conflict, but at the expense of possibly some good ideas. It seems like this is what happened at your last Lead Team meeting. I would suggest, based on how this meeting goes, that you might want to do another coaching/mentoring session with Meghan."

"Dalton," Matt continued, "we have another situation for you to keep in mind. Jim Franklin, our IT Audit Director, is an expert with technology and he really understands IT risks and controls. However, he's really bad at the people stuff and does not seem to want, or care, to get any better. I've coached him several times, but he just does not seem to understand others or even want to understand what motivates them. Jim is usually baffled when an interaction goes wrong. I inherited him from my predecessor, and confidentially, I'm thinking hard about trying to arrange a transfer to one of the IT areas where he can work mostly by himself and his computers. He and Linda Hernandez, our IT Audit Manager, don't get along at all. Linda, while not nearly as strong technically as Jim, is much more in tune with people. Our staff and clients love Linda and try to avoid Jim. At audit exit meetings with our auditees, I see Linda visibly cringe at how Jim words things. Frankly, I cringe myself. Handling this situation is beyond the scope of our session this morning, but I wanted you to be aware of this possible conflict."

With this, Matt seemed to run out of words and Dalton commented, "Yeah, I've seen the tension around Jim. Let me ask, if you move Jim out, could Linda step in as the IT Audit Director now?"

Matt paused, making sure he was being fair to Linda. "She's great, but I just promoted her six months ago to Manager, and she probably needs more development and experience. If I promote her too fast, she would end up with a much higher risk of failure. There are things she still needs to learn. She has great potential and I really want to help her so she's ready to be the IT director. If I move Jim out, I would likely need to hire somebody over Linda. I'm considering giving Linda the responsibility for leading the development of a new audit discipline with a team. This should help grow her leadership skills. I am still thinking about this, but I plan to engage you with this new development team. Listen, this situation will not be resolved this afternoon. I haven't completely given up on Jim, and maybe as you see him operate, you can give me your thoughts."

Dalton's immediate response was, "That is what I am here for!"—one of his favorite expressions.

Matt was about to hang up when he remembered he had another item to cover with Dalton. He fleetingly thought of Detective Colombo's favorite line: "One more thing." "I also wanted to let you know I plan to keep very quiet during our session today, so don't be surprised. I really want to observe how Meghan, Jim, and the international managers do without much of a signal from me. If they know what risks I consider most important, they may not be as free to generate new ideas. This is a bright group and I'm sure they will think of things I haven't considered. If, toward the end of our session, I believe we didn't get to all the right set of risks for next year, I'll jump in. So, I'll see you at 10:00 A.M.!"

Dalton thought to himself that this was one of the first rules of avoiding Groupthink: having management purposely quiet during group discussions to assist in soliciting everyone's thoughts. Dalton replied with a quick, "I understand, Matt, see you soon," and both hung up their phones.

· · ·

An hour later, Dalton was graphically cursing to himself as the Chicago traffic slowed him to a crawl. He had a meeting with Matt and his management team in 20 minutes, and he knew Matt was a stickler for punctuality. He was also on the phone with his ex-wife, struggling to coordinate weekends with the kids. He was still mourning the end of his marriage, but both agreed it was for the best. At least it was an amicable split. Both were working very hard to make sure their kids were loved and had as normal a life as possible.

He finally rushed into the MultiCrown audit conference room a bit out of breath, with a bead of sweat trickling down his cleanly shaven head. "Good morning, everybody. I'm sorry I'm a few minutes late!" Dalton exclaimed in his loud and cheerful voice.

Matt replied in a gracious tone: "Hi, Dalton, no worries; we were just having coffee and getting reconnected with our international team." Matt indicated each of his management team members as he spoke. "I'm sure you remember Meghan Dorsch, our Audit Director; Jim Franklin, our IT Audit Director; Linda Hernandez, our IT Audit Manager; and our Financial and Operational Audit Managers, Bill Dorset and Lee Akisodo. And of course, you remember Lila." Matt smiled to himself, knowing how Dalton felt about his executive assistant;

however, with a newly divorced Dalton, and knowing his personality, he would not be surprised if he felt similarly toward many women. Dalton gave a friendly nod to each person as Matt reintroduced them and lingered and smiled deeply at Lila.

Matt continued, "Since the purpose of today's meeting is to work on our risk assessment for next year, we brought in our audit managers from each of our three international satellite audit offices for this session and also for several other meetings this week. They already know about you and the nature of your People-Centric (P-C) work with us. This is Sandra Moliterno, the Audit Manager in our Sao Paulo, Brazil, office."

Dalton almost succeeded in keeping cool while meeting the stunning and vivacious Sandra, but by now, Matt was able to read Dalton pretty well by his facial expressions and body language. Dalton's pupils also appreciably dilated, indicating his intense concentration and interest in Sandra. Matt also knew Dalton well enough to understand that his body language was being utilized very purposefully. However, Matt knew that regardless of how much Dalton was on the prowl after his divorce, he would remain professional in the office. What they did after hours was their business. He did have some concern about a possible conflict between Sandra and Lila, but then, Matt always seemed to have something or somebody to worry about, which was probably a good attribute in his job as "chief worrier" for MultiCrown.

Matt then turned to a short, roundish gentleman with a beard. "This is Luis Rocha, our Audit Manager in Madrid, Spain." Matt then indicated with his hand at a very dignified and thin Asian gentleman, and said, "This is Ivan Leong; he's the Audit Manager over our Singapore audit team."

As Matt was introducing his team, Dalton warmly shook hands with each in turn.

Matt sat back in his chair, crossed his legs and sipped some coffee from his ever-present mug, and exclaimed, "Let's get this show on the road. We've a lot to cover today to get our risk assessment and next year's audit plan started. Dalton and I discussed how we might go about this and decided we would start with a brainstorming session to generate as many ideas as possible, and then we'll Multivote and have further discussions to narrow the list to the top risks we see for next year. Once we have our initial list, we'll need to have good discussions with operating and executive management to hear their concerns and get their input. Of course, the Audit Committee will need to give the final approval. Dalton will explain these tools and facilitate our discussion."

Dalton began to elaborate on the general objectives and rules of brainstorming, in addition to providing a background on Groupthink. "As most of you are aware, brainstorming is a very effective way of considering ideas from different perspectives. Brainstorming is basically used when a group of people meet to *creatively* generate new ideas around a specific area of interest. Brainstorming rules remove barriers, which enables people to think more freely, explore new areas of thought, and so create numerous new ideas and solutions. Here are some of the general rules we should follow today:

"Everyone should call out ideas as they occur to them. *Every* idea is written down, regardless if they might seem unusual, or even bizarre. In our case, Lila will take notes on her laptop and project them for all to see. It's okay to build on the ideas raised by others to generate variations of ideas.

"All the ideas, no matter how unusual they may be, are included and *are not to be criticized* by anybody. This is the hardest rule for some people to follow, especially for auditors! However, this rule is absolutely essential. If people are afraid of being criticized, they may hold back some of the most creative and valuable ideas.

"However, it's fine if everyone asks real, nonjudgmental clarification questions to understand the ideas. Please be careful how you word these so that it doesn't come across as criticism. Watch your use of emotional or trigger words.

"Only when the brainstorming session is over are the ideas evaluated, combined, changed if necessary, or deleted. Everybody on the team needs to participate. If I see you holding back, I'll draw you out, but it's better if you're actively contributing.

"The loudest and most aggressive talkers need to be careful they don't overshadow the others and generate quick, but incomplete or wrong solutions. I may gently remind you to let others speak."

Dalton slowly lingered on this last statement and stared, ever so slightly, in Meghan's general vicinity before he continued.

"There are no 'ranks' in a brainstorming session. Everybody should be considered equal. In our case, Matt and I agreed that he'll mostly listen through the brainstorming session so as to not apply any distorting influence.

"We keep going until everybody runs out of ideas and we start to repeat ourselves. Are these rules clear to everybody?" Dalton looked around the room to make sure there were no questions.

He then continued: "What we must watch out for is Groupthink. I don't believe it will be too prevalent with this group since all of you are very experienced and outspoken, but let's at least discuss the concept in general. Groupthink is when someone thinks about raising an issue or a question in a group setting, but then refrains because he or she is afraid others might disagree and does not want to destroy the group harmony."

At this point, Matt commented, "I'm sure all of you, as managers, have been frustrated at one time or another when you knew an auditor had ideas, but was reluctant to rock the boat. Sometimes it feels like you are pulling teeth to get real thoughts from somebody!" As he looked around the room, almost everybody nodded, or ruefully smiled, acknowledging this observation.

Dalton, pleased by this addition from Matt, paused a minute. "We need to be careful, because some of the ways to avoid Groupthink violate the brainstorming rules, particularly about not criticizing the ideas of other people. The thing to remember is this: *While* we are brainstorming, we follow the brainstorming rules and accept all suggestions, but later on, when actively deciding what to select, you need to watch out for Groupthink. This could be a bit confusing, so let me give you a few suggestions on *avoiding* Groupthink and we can discuss afterwards.

"This doesn't apply now since I'm covering the concepts with you, but make sure you explain what Groupthink is if the people in your group are not familiar with it. You can then acknowledge that Groupthink could occur. Everybody needs to understand they have to be *willing* to explore different scenarios before you settle on a decision. We make our greatest mistakes by running with the first solution or idea and not exploring all alternative scenarios.

"Encourage each member of the team to be a critical evaluator, allowing them to openly question ideas and propose alternatives. *Make it safe for everyone to do so.*

"Leaders should deliberately not express their opinion up front when asking a group to find a solution to a problem, just as Matt is planning on doing today—if he can contain himself!

"If the decision is critical enough, we could have several different groups solve the same problem simultaneously, but independently of each other. We could also assign at least one group member to deliberately play the role of 'devil's advocate' and purposefully challenge the various decisions."

Dalton looked around to see how the group was reacting to the rules and commented, "Let me pause a minute before going into our brainstorming session. Are there any questions or comments about these?"

Linda hesitated a bit before she commented, "So, let me get it straight. Basically, *during* brainstorming, we all suggest ideas, even very *creative, maybe a bit off-the-wall.* Nobody should criticize any idea based on the brainstorming rules, and nobody should be afraid of suggesting any idea based on the *avoiding* Groupthink suggestions. Then, later on, as we are out of brainstorming mode and we are discussing the various ideas to narrow our list to the best items, we again need to follow the Avoiding Groupthink rules. Is that right?"

As Dalton looked around, he noticed everybody nodding thoughtfully at Linda's concise summary. "Linda, you've got it exactly right. We need to balance the brainstorming rules and the Avoiding Groupthink rules, and they each come to the front at different times in the decision process. Once people are familiar with both sets of rules, it's very natural to do, but at the beginning it may feel a bit awkward. Again, the thing to remember for this next session is to suggest *all* your ideas without worrying about what others might think, and if you hear an idea you don't agree with, you don't criticize it during the brainstorming process. Also, watch your facial expressions and body language. It's easy to physically criticize without even knowing it!" He again paused to see if there were any additional comments, but nobody else said anything.

Dalton said, "All right, everyone, let's begin. This discussion is all about your risk assessment for next year and eventually, creating your audit plan. Where do you think we should start?"

Meghan chimed in and forcefully started to talk about what they audited last year and the most painful risks they tackled. As Matt had pointed out privately, Meghan has the most aggressive personality in the team, and Dalton wanted to make sure she did not steamroll the others. It was hard to not let Meghan speak; she has an air of confidence that is rare. Dalton respectfully cut her off and stated, "Instead of thinking about last year's risks, let us think more broadly and start with a blank slate. If we focus on prior risks, we'll repeat many of the same audits as last year, which might be appropriate, but we can come to that conclusion later in this process. You must continue to evolve as an audit shop and consider new risks. What is the definition of *insanity?* According to Einstein, a pretty smart fellow, insanity is doing the same thing over and over and expecting a different result. If we continue to look back, we will never make progress."

This was a way for Dalton to moderate Meghan's strong voice, since unchecked, the group could fall into Groupthink and unknowingly go along with what she pushed. Dalton looked at Meghan to see if he stepped on her too hard, but decided she was okay. In fact, she smiled knowingly at him, probably understanding what he was trying to do.

"Instead of looking back, let's look forward with an open mind. What are the key risks to this organization? What are the new initiatives that we are undertaking and where does management feel we are, regarding MultiCrown's risk appetite?"

The group was silent, with nobody seeming to want to break the ice. To get them thinking in a broader, more open manner, Dalton added: "Here is another question we should ask ourselves, and this is personally one of my favorites since it's the basis for auditing, but, as internal auditors, we tend to overlook this key point, so let me ask: What is the overall objective of internal auditing in an organization?"

Matt smiled at this question since he was not sure his team would get this answer without some prodding.

Sandra and Luis from Sao Paulo huddled for a few seconds, and finally Luis stated, "We are to assist the organization in its compliance efforts in regard to rules and regulations."

Bill chimed in, leaning forward, and said, "Yes, we have a focus on Sarbanes-Oxley (SOX) compliance."

Ivan, the auditor from Singapore, sat very upright in his chair, with perfect posture, leaned forward slightly, and stated: "I agree, but are we not focusing on *just* compliance with rules and regulations; how about company policy and procedures?"

Dalton smiled at Ivan, nodding his head approvingly. "Ivan, I agree with you and everyone else so far, but you guys are thinking like *auditors*! Stop thinking like auditors and start thinking through a risk-based lens: What is the *objective* of internal audit?"

Meghan continued to shift in her chair uncomfortably. She didn't want to be embarrassed in front of the group, and as Matt had advised her after the last audit manager meeting, she needed to give everyone an opportunity to speak, but finally she could not contain herself. She uncrossed her legs, jotted down a few notes and decided to chime in. "I agree with everyone, but isn't one of our main goals to improve the efficiency and effectiveness of MultiCrown?"

Again, Dalton nodded approvingly. "Great point Meghan, but keep going." The team seemed a bit mystified and somewhat apprehensive about continuing the conversation. It was evident to Dalton that there was definitely some Groupthink in the team and Meghan was causing it, at least unconsciously. Unsure of what Dalton meant, Meghan did not respond.

After a few awkward moments, Dalton changed direction and read Lila's body language. He smiled thoughtfully and said, "Lila, I know you are not an auditor per se, but what are your thoughts?" She hesitated, so Dalton continued, "Lila, I know, based on your physical shifting, twiddling of your hands, and facial expressions, that you have plenty to say right now; don't worry, I think a new perspective would be very helpful."

Lila, overcoming a slight bout of shyness, said, "I might not be an auditor but I think I have a pretty good feel for our business. Regardless, in every business, all employees are there to do one main central thing—help the company meet its objectives and goals."

Dalton smiled broadly as this was exactly what he was looking for. "Folks, this is a perfect example of a new perspective adding significant value to the audit process. Lila's 100 percent right—you all were correct, also, but the root objective of audit and all departments is to continue to contribute to the organization to meet its objectives. We tend to forget it, but our clients definitely remember this. If we continue to remind our clients that we have the same objective, it should help us be considered part of the team and signal that we want the best for MultiCrown." As Dalton looked at the team, he saw nods of understanding and agreement from all. Matt had an appreciative smile on his face.

From this high note, the team dove into a deep, two-hour session to generate key audit risks and opportunities for MultiCrown. Reminding everybody of the purpose of Internal Audit had been a bit of side discussion, but set the stage for the types of areas that Internal Audit could help with and assisted the group by spurring a lively discussion.

Jim and Linda, the IT audit leaders, started with the obvious key risk in the organization: SAP system implementations. For years, MultiCrown was on numerous disparate systems. Since 2011, they have been implementing SAP throughout the organization. As with any significant system implementation, there had been many bumps, cost overages, and delays, but the project was back on track for now. As Dalton listened to Jim and Linda go back and forth, he could sense the tense energy in both of their voices.

With a bit of nonverbal prompting by Dalton, Sandra used an opening to bring up the significant increase in risk regarding a bevy of areas overseas, including compliance with the U.S. Foreign Corrupt Practices Act (FCPA) and other anticorruption risks; hedging and derivatives; the new Payables Shared Services in South America; and finally, several new acquisitions. Meanwhile, as Sandra was speaking, Lila added each idea into the "bulleted" brainstorming list she was projecting on the screen.

Dalton, ever-mindful of other's body language, began to notice how ridiculous his own was at that moment. He was leaning forward, staring into Sandra's eyes intently, and utilizing active listening skills for her to recognize that she was, at that moment, the only person in the room. He realized it might become obvious to the rest of the room that he was a bit smitten, and pulled back to encompass the entire group in the discussion.

Sandra, well aware of her impact on Dalton and what he was probably thinking, and not seeming to mind, elaborated on her ideas: "Based on what I've seen at our division, these are all very significant risks. With the new laws around bribery and corruption, we in Brazil are still learning, as a country, how to control this area. Hedging will probably always be a concern as the lack of training and understanding is evident in our walkthroughs. No?"

She continued, "Finally, we've struggled with massive change, which I don't believe is anything unique to our division specifically. With the South America Shared Services for Accounts Payables coming online next year, in addition to new acquisitions on the horizon, I'm worried that the South American audit group will be spread very thin." You could see the tension on Sandra's face. Her lips were pursed, her legs crossed tightly, and her brow was tending downward in the middle. She was exhibiting all the telltale cluster signs of nervousness or tension.

Matt was about to speak up to address Sandra's concerns, but looked at Dalton first. He was able to read Dalton's expression and recalled that groups could fall into Groupthink based on management's signals. So, instead of commenting, he let the conversation continue.

After a short break, Linda Hernandez started a discussion of cyber-attacks and hacking. Linda's background was in cyber-security and she was very enthusiastic about the subject. Everyone could sense, based on her tone of voice and upright posture, that this was one of her true passions. "People are naturally reactive; organizations need to continually strive to be more proactive. We must become more engaged and convince our IT organization that these areas are a significant concern. If not, and I know we tend to overuse the term, we have significant 'reputation risk' for our organization."

During Linda's comments, Jim's body language changed. His chin went up and he continued to slightly shake his head in disagreement. His arms and legs were both crossed, denoting a lack of openness. As he sat next to Linda, he continued to lean toward her, to a point where it appeared he might get uncomfortably close. Here was another telltale nonverbal attempt to intimidate. He would only look in her general direction, never making eye contact. Jim's body language matched his attitude and demeanor. He was very defensive and not clearly on the same page as Linda. In fact, he was extremely argumentative and thought the focus of IT should be on the new IT infrastructure and its related demands. Everyone could tell this was a hot button item for both of them and that this was not the first public argument on the subject and probably not the last.

Dalton pointed out to the group in general, but really to Jim, "Everybody, please remember the rules of brainstorming call for all ideas to be included and not criticized at the time they are suggested." Throughout the heated discussion between Linda and Jim, Lila was very skillfully pulling out the individual risks mentioned by both and impartially adding them to the bulleted list on the screen. This was her way of following the brainstorming rules and supporting the team.

Dalton noticed the additions to the list and reinforced Lila's actions. "Lila, I'm glad you are putting down all the ideas at this brainstorming stage. You are doing a great job with this!" Lila smiled broadly at this compliment from Dalton.

Bill Dorset, the Financial/Operational Audit Manager, then brought up the recurring topic of SOX Compliance. "Look, maybe everyone doesn't value SOX, but it's still a very relevant risk inside this organization." He continued: "Any type of compliance efforts are key risks from a shareholder's standpoint, in my opinion. This includes our revised safety initiatives in our plants throughout the world."

Meghan rolled her eyes and whispered what appeared to be a snide comment at Jim. Then she said to the whole group, "Look, SOX is still relevant, but we've not had any significant issues in four years; it's embedded in the fabric of the organization. To still call this a major risk would be an overstatement!"

Dalton noted to himself that Meghan couldn't seem to abide by the rules of brainstorming. Dalton could sense that the life was being sucked out of the room with each comment Meghan made. It seemed as if she wanted to make sure everyone knew she was the smartest person in the room and definitely second in command. She surely did not realize how it made her appear the exact opposite. Dalton thought she was probably insecure in her role, as Matt had suggested earlier. As Dalton looked at Matt, he could see the worried look on his face as he also concluded that Meghan was damaging the team dynamics.

Surprisingly, Bill did not back down and this impressed Dalton. "Meghan, we've been very fortunate in having strong leadership and a great tone at the top here at MultiCrown. SOX *is* embedded into the fabric of the organization; I agree. However, we have to make sure that emphasis continues. What if a big financial reporting problem did come up after years of great compliance? How would this reflect on MultiCrown *and* Internal Audit? Finally, much of what we've spoken about already ties into SOX compliance in some way or another." Everyone nodded approvingly at Bill standing up to Meghan. With a deep frown, Meghan, shaking her head sourly, stared down at her lap—maybe at her phone. She presented a rude body language and a clear indication of her disagreement with Bill's suggestions.

Lee Akisodo, a very distinguished and calm man, seemed a bit put out by all of the heated discussion between the team members. Dalton had been observing his subtle but attentive listening throughout the day. Dalton could sense that Lee had comments on the discussions but continued to only listen and take notes. Dalton had considered calling on him specifically, but Lee, in a formal manner, finally chimed in. "Everyone, this has been a great session so far. There have been some excellent points made and I appreciate everyone's ideas. I have a few comments to add, if I may do so now." Lee politely looked around to see if there were any objections, looked down at his notes and then calmly continued. "With the significant economic shifts we've experienced over the past four years, and with the MultiCrown CFO focusing on decreasing cost by 8 percent next year, operational audits should be a significant focus for us. I guess the risk is of not meeting MultiCrown's cost-cutting objectives, but I see it more as an *opportunity* to help Management improve operationally."

Lee continued, "Additionally, the work we are currently performing around Supply Chain Management, to understand the business drivers of the area, is also very important. Lastly, I also believe the new customer fulfillment system and processes will be of high risk as change drives uncertainty and risk. Jim and Linda, would you agree on the systems risk?" Jim and Linda both nodded approvingly with some of the team surprised they can agree on anything.

Dalton responded, "Lee, great suggestions! We'll be sure to capture them." He then looked to Lila, but given her competence, he unnecessarily confirmed she was already recording the new ideas.

Dalton noted that Luis was very quiet at the meeting and somewhat reluctant to participate. During the breaks, he was very friendly and outgoing with the others, so he was not antisocial. While his grammar in English was school-perfect, he spoke with a heavy Spanish accent and was not too familiar with American colloquialisms. Dalton amusingly remembered his puzzled look when Linda told him "she was as happy as a clam." He committed to drawing Luis out since he probably just needed a bit of encouragement to get over any embarrassment about his accent.

Dalton continued watching Meghan's reaction to everyone at the meeting as she wore her emotions on her sleeve. Meghan, during Lee's comments, constantly shifted in her chair and looked away. He surmised that perhaps Meghan lacked confidence in the other managers and resisted hearing much from them. Dalton, with a touch of jealousy, also observed the constant back-and-forth between Sandra and Luis; it did seem that this was a bit more than co-workers chatting, but maybe he was imagining it. Maybe it was closeness due to their having a non-U.S. culture in common—Brazil and Spain.

With Dalton instilling more confidence in her throughout the day, Lila added a few comments on the importance of fraud and how MultiCrown might see an increase with the tough economic times. Dalton just smiled broadly; Lila did the same.

The discussion continued, and everybody was now actively engaged in generating ideas. There were a few further heated exchanges between the IT and the financial auditors on which risks were more critical at this time. Dalton struggled to keep the brainstorming rules in effect by not letting the criticism by some members of the team derail the others from contributing their thoughts. He used his wit and humor to continue to deflect any heated comments.

The team, after this great discussion, began to wrap up and finally, after hours of silence, and more importantly, observation, Matt decided it was time to chime in. Matt sat up in his chair a little after noon and enthusiastically stated: "Okay, team, it has been a very productive morning. We accomplished a lot. All the high risks I had in mind, plus many more, have been suggested by you, although I had to work hard to button my lips at times. I'm sure you know how hard it is to keep my opinions to myself!" They all smiled at this, either in understanding, or to signal the boss they appreciated his sense of humor. "To summarize, we brainstormed 68 separate risks and opportunities after we weeded out duplications and combined similar items. Of course, we can't take this many items to the Audit Committee and Executive Management. While I believe most of the 68 risks and opportunities are generally valid, they are not all equally important. We'll need to narrow the list so we can focus our audit resources where they count the most."

Matt continued: "As Dalton pointed out, brainstorming is a great way to generate many creative ideas without any restraining barriers. However, a downside of brainstorming is that ideas get on the list without much meaningful discussion or critical thinking. As we mentioned when we kicked off our session, Dalton and I agreed that after our brainstorming session we would utilize Multivoting to help us narrow the list to the most critical risks and opportunities. I think somewhere in the ballpark of 15 would be the right number that we can highlight for the Audit Committee and Executive Management. The Audit Committee is interested in the big picture and having too many items on the list may reduce their focus on the *key* risks. Based on their comments last year, when I presented 25 items, I think the top 15 risks/opportunities would be their preference."

Matt turned to Lila. "Do you know if our box-lunches arrived? We are at a good stopping point."

Lila stepped out to check and returned right away, addressing everyone. "The box-lunches and drinks are here—how about if you all head to the kitchen and bring back the box with your name on it?" A few minutes later they all sat around the conference table investigating the contents of their boxes. Matt, a huge fan of chocolate-chip cookies, discreetly waved his cookie at Dalton and they both nodded with mock solemnity. They all started a friendly and lively discussion, mostly focusing on drawing out the international audit managers and catching up on personal news since they last got together.

After lunch, Matt said, "How about if we take a break from our meeting so we can catch up on any critical emails and then get back together at two o'clock? We can then begin our Multivoting session."

Right on time, they all straggled back to the conference room, and Dalton began to outline the next steps.

"As Matt mentioned before lunch, we need to narrow our long list down to a manageable number of the most important risks and opportunities. One technique that is commonly used to do this after a brainstorming session is called *Multivoting*. Multivoting is preferable over regular voting because it allows an item that is *favored by most of the team*, but not necessarily the *top* choice of any one team member, to be included in the list.

"There are a variety of ways to do Multivoting, but let's keep it as simple as possible. Something we already did before lunch was to review our initial long brainstorming list and combine similar items. As I'm sure you remember, this took quite a bit of time and discussion, but I'm glad we were able to do so. Now we have the 68 distinct risks. Lila was kind enough to number the items from 1 to 68. They are not in any order of priority; the list is in the order in which the items were suggested. She also printed out the list for each of us." Dalton uttered this with his ever-present smile toward Lila.

"Our next step is for each of you to vote privately on your copy. Vote for the 23 items that you feel we should focus on next year. Twenty-three is about a third of the 68 items, and this ratio is typical in a round of Multivoting. Look beyond your own area of expertise and list the items you really feel are the most important ones to MultiCrown. If an item was on the original brainstorming list, but there is really no broad support for the item, then that item may get a vote from the person who proposed it, but not other votes. Multivoting would quickly weed out this narrow suggestion during the first round.

"Please take 20 minutes or so to select your 23 items."

While the team was working, Dalton went to the kitchen to get a cup of coffee, pleasantly surprised to see the pot had a decaffeinated hazelnut-flavored blend. He definitely did not need to be more hyped-up than he already was. He was excited about the progress so far and greatly anticipated a good scotch-on-the-rocks before dinner.

Returning to the conference room, Dalton gave the team a few more minutes until he saw everybody looking up. "Okay, are you ready for the next step?" When everybody nodded, he continued. "As we go around the room, each of you should in turn call out the numbers, from 1 to 68, corresponding to the items you voted for. Lila can then, on her laptop, add a tick-mark next to each item you call out. This should only take a few minutes."

As the team members went around the room giving Lila their votes, Dalton let his eyes roam back and forth between Lila and Sandra. Matt caught his eyes and gave him a knowing smile. Dalton, a bit abashed, looked down for a second, but then continued to look at Sandra and Lila. Matt amusedly thought that Dalton was not the type to stay abashed for long.

When all the votes were in, Dalton turned to Lila and asked her if she could sort the list by the number of votes received, keeping the original identifying number of each item. With Lila's experienced use of Excel, she was able to come to the answer quickly. "Lila, how many items received more than two votes?" Lila looked down at her laptop and responded: "Twenty-nine." Everybody looked at the screen with great interest where Lila had projected the sorted list.

Dalton then explained: "Everyone, this is very typical in Multivoting; a number of rounds of voting may be needed to get to the desired shortlist. Following the Multivoting guidelines, you each should vote on 10 items from the 29 selected in the last round—again, about a third of the list. However, before we do so, this is an opportunity for all of you to make a pitch for any items you really believe belong in the top 15. However, don't just rehash what was said earlier. If you have additional logic or facts to support your items, please let the rest know your thoughts. This is a good time for us to view the items in a critical fashion."

The team spent another hour or so as the various members argued to have their pet risks and opportunities included in the shortlist. Being experienced auditors, they were very good at rational arguments and facts, and the discussion took place in a relatively calm and harmonious manner.

Finally, Dalton interceded. "Okay, it looks like everybody has had their say. So, go ahead and take 15 more minutes for each of you to allocate your 10 votes and then give them to Lila for the next round." While the votes took place, Dalton pulled out his pad to catch up on emails, a constant barrage he always fought against. He also checked in on the sports news and anything else he has missed out on today. He needed the mental break.

As Dalton looked up, he saw that Lila had finished tabulating and resorting the list. Before he could ask, she anticipated him and exclaimed: "We have 12 items with more than four votes, and 18 items with three or more votes."

Dalton seemed pleased with this. "We have a couple of ways to get to 15. We can take the 12 with four or more votes and have Matt select the other three risks. Alternatively, I recommend we open up the floor and again let anybody make an impassioned plea to include any item that was passed over in the prior voting rounds. We can discuss any proposal you all have, and either let Matt decide then, or do another round of Multivoting to get the additional three items. What do you think Matt?"

After thinking a bit, Matt replied, "Let's have each person make a case for including an item that we didn't select in the prior round, and we can discuss it. This way we can add intelligent discussions for items on the boundary. Yes, I realize this might take some more time, but I think this is a valuable discussion. I think all the items with four votes seem pretty firm to me. After our discussions, I'll then use my managerial prerogative to decide which additional three items to include. As the person responsible to communicate the list to the Audit Committee and the CEO, I may need to tweak all the items after I think about them for a few days. Ultimately, this is my job, although I really appreciate having your thoughtful input."

Dalton looked up and stated, "Okay, let's do it that way. Who has a burning need to champion an item we skipped?"

Before his words were out, Sandra excitedly said, "Listen, we did not include the Brazil Payables Shared Services for South America. This is a very important area, no? We pay over 400 million U.S. dollars in invoices in South America, and we really need to make sure these new Shared Services controls are working!"

Most of the rest of the team nodded thoughtfully, and then Linda jumped in. "I can't believe we didn't include the cyber-attack risks on our list! With all the hackers out there, not to mention the state-sponsored cyber-attacks, we are very vulnerable. Not only could an attack really harm MultiCrown, but we in audit would look pretty foolish if we did not have this on our radar!"

Dalton noted Matt's almost-imperceptible nod, and figured Linda had made her case.

At this point Meghan excitedly exclaimed: "It's true that cyber-security is a high 'inherent risk,' but I really feel the IT organization has this one well under control, so the residual risk is not really that high." Dalton observed that since the team was out of the brainstorming stage, Meghan's critical comments were really appropriate to avoid Groupthink. The criticism was even stated politely.

Another 40 minutes went by, and everyone had had their say and they were starting to repeat themselves. Dalton exclaimed, "Okay, great! I'm very pleased at how you all participated and that you mostly 'played nicely' with each other according to the brainstorming rules. Also, I think you ultimately avoided Groupthink. As far as I could tell, nobody held back any ideas to avoid conflicts." He looked around to observe any signs that he was wrong about this, and modestly concluded that once again he was right. "Matt, do you have enough to complete the list of 15 risks?"

Matt replied: "Why don't you all take a 10-minute break and I'll work on Lila's laptop to finalize the list?" With that, he bent over the laptop and quickly started to type on the risk/opportunity list using only about six or seven fingers. During the break, Dalton spoke to everyone, planning an impromptu happy hour. Some extra bonding over a few drinks would help the team.

By the end of the break, Matt had projected the updated list on the whiteboard. They all stared at it with mixed feelings. Brainstorming and

Multivoting are good processes to generate many ideas and narrow them down afterwards, but some people's favorite ideas can get skipped.

When Matt asked, "What do you all think about this list?" he was pleasantly surprised when Meghan quietly said, "This may not be everything I would have included in a top 15 list, but I felt the process did capture everybody's input in a fair and systematic manner. I think we generated a very good list that reflected all of our ideas. At least you now have our collective thoughts as you firm up the risks. I have to say, I started out being very skeptical about this process, but we really did get good results." Dalton continued to change his opinion of Meghan; perhaps he needed to reconsider his initial conclusions on her. Matt certainly believed that Meghan could eventually become a very valuable member of his team. However, she was a pain at times.

With that positive statement, most of the team nodded in agreement. Some people seemed puzzled, but pleasantly surprised by Meghan's change in attitude.

Proposed Top Audit Risks/Opportunities for MultiCrown for Next Year (Not in Priority Order—Draft)

1. SAP system implementations in Asia, Texas, and Germany—Risk
2. FCPA/Anticorruption compliance, primarily in Argentina, Asia, UK, and Russia—Risk
3. Meeting the 8 percent goal to cut MultiCrown global cost set by new CFO—Opportunity
4. Hedging/Derivatives—U.S., Europe, and South America—Risk
5. Cyber-attacks—global concern—Risk
6. Cloud-computing initiatives—Opportunity/Risk
7. New IT infrastructure—Risk
8. Significant fraud events—Risk
9. SOX compliance—Risk
10. Supply Chain Rationalization Project—Opportunity
11. New repair and maintenance processes/systems—Opportunity
12. Contract management in the Material Design Services business—Opportunity
13. MultiCrown's safety goals (TBD) for next year—Risk
14. New Payables Shared Services in Brazil—Risk (maybe some Opportunity)
15. Assimilation of acquisitions in India, Chile, and Alabama—Risk/Opportunity

A little past 5:30 P.M., after a long, hard, but very productive day, Matt called a halt to the meeting. "Luis and Ivan are probably jet-lagged from crossing so many time zones and might want to turn in early, but please let me know if you would like to go out tonight for dinner. Sandra, you still seem very lively, but of course Sao Paulo and Chicago are in the same time zone."

At this point, Dalton quickly jumped in and sheepishly said: "Well, actually, I asked the team to join me for a cocktail and possibly dinner afterwards at Rosebud on Rush Street—they have great Italian food. Does anybody else want to come along?" Dalton was mostly focused on having dinner with Sandra. The invitation to the team for dinner was said in a halfhearted manner, and it was obvious he wanted to get to know Sandra better *without* others around.

Matt cynically thought that Dalton was at some point very likely to suggest a trip to Brazil to work on the "serious" interpersonal issues down there. Lila seemed to be put out by the obvious interest Dalton was showing Sandra, and an observant Matt thought to himself that this could lead to an interesting situation. With that, the auditors dispersed and agreed to meet next morning at 8:00 A.M. to continue work on a draft of their audit plans for next year.

Dalton stayed behind for a few minutes to debrief. "Matt, how do you think it went?"

Matt took his usual moment to properly arrange his thoughts and responded, "I think we went through the structured brainstorming and Multivoting processes very well. I'm not too worried about Groupthink at this point; everybody seemed comfortable contributing their ideas. I'm really pleased with our final results. Our list of the top 15 risks and opportunities that Audit can tackle are really right on point from my perspective. The discussions were rich and very productive, and I think this will help us be on the same page about our main areas of focus for next year's audit coverage. I'm sure that Management and the Audit Committee will have additional thoughts, but I'm confident I could justify and defend these 15 items. I thought your facilitation was great!"

Dalton nodded at the compliment and asked, "What about Meghan?" Matt again thought for several moments before he replied, "I am not sure; I could have strangled her at times. When you reminded her of the brainstorming rule against criticism, she seemed to accept it for a while, but then she reverted back. I was surprised at the positive way she ended the session. My guess is she realized she had not handled herself well during the day."

"If you are aware of your own interpersonal deficiency, it is a huge step toward resolving the problem. Acknowledgment is the first step toward improvement." Dalton was quoting from his own training material.

"I really want her to succeed," Matt said. "She's very smart and I think she'll be able to turn this around. She spent her entire career prior to

MultiCrown in a very confrontational corporate culture. Over there, you either attacked or you were attacked. The reason she left was partly because she wanted a warmer, more supportive culture. I think she needs to be mentored to help her understand that our culture is really different. She's also somewhat unsure of her role here, and I need to help her change without aggravating the lack-of-confidence issue. I think I will take her to lunch in a few days to see if I can get through to her in a more convivial setting. Food always helps!"

Dalton nodded wisely and turned to leave. Just as he was going through the door, he heard Matt say, "Have a good time tonight with Sandra!" Dalton continued with a big grin on his face, but did not turn around. He *really* did not want Matt asking him if his intentions were honorable.

People-Centric Skills Highlighted in This Chapter

Groupthink

DEFINITION

When a member of a team thinks about raising an issue or question in a group meeting, but then refrains because he's afraid others might disagree and does not want to destroy the cohesion.

Leading Practices—Avoiding Groupthink

1. Be willing to explore different scenarios before settling on a decision.

2. Encourage each member of the team to be a critical evaluator, allowing them to openly question ideas and propose alternatives.

3. Leaders should deliberately not express their opinion up front when asking a group to find a solution to a problem.

4. Invite outside experts into the meeting and take their opinions seriously. Allow the group members to speak with the experts individually and privately if they desire.

5. If the decision is major enough, instruct several different groups to solve the same problem simultaneously, but independently, of each other.

6. Assign at least one group member to deliberately play the role of devil's advocate.

Brainstorming

DEFINITION

Brainstorming is a group creativity technique by which efforts are made to find a conclusion for a specific problem by gathering the most comprehensive list of ideas spontaneously contributed by the group members.

Brainstorming Rules

1. **Defer judgment.** Don't block someone else's idea, even if you don't like it. Put it on the list; the team may be able to build on it later. Don't criticize or challenge the others' thoughts, even if it's only with body language.

2. **Go for volume.** Getting to 50 ideas is better than 10, no matter what you initially think about the quality of the suggestions.

3. **Conduct only one conversation at a time.** When different conversations are going on within a team, no one can focus. Do not interrupt or talk over each other.

4. **Build on the ideas of others.** This leverages the perspective of diverse team members and can be especially useful when you feel like you're stuck.

5. **Stay on topic.** One possible tool is to have a "Parking Lot" for ideas people have, but that don't fit the topic at hand. These ideas can be considered in a separate session. An advantage of this is that you don't get into a mode of criticizing an idea because it does not fit the topic. Criticism is the enemy of brainstorming.

6. **Encourage wild ideas.** The more unique the better; you never know where your team might be able to take them. One way to do this is to remove constraints to get more creativity. For example, state that at this time, next year's budget is not a factor, and see if this generates further suggestions.

Multivoting

PURPOSE

This tool helps narrow a long list down to a manageable number of the most important items. Multivoting is usually used after a brainstorming session that produced a long set of possibilities that need to be whittled down. Multivoting is also a consensus-building tool, where the decision on the final list of items is made by group involvement and judgment. The purpose of Multivoting is not to have a unanimous

(continued)

vote. Instead, Multivoting aims at reaching a consensus, even if the final items don't represent every participant's first choice. Multivoting is more effective than regular voting because it allows an item that is favored by most of the team, but is not necessarily the top choice of any one group member.

PROCEDURE

1. Display the list of options (from brainstorming or other idea-generating methodology).

2. Review each item to make sure everyone in the group understands it. Combine duplicate or similar items. Number all items sequentially.

3. Decide how many items each person should vote on from the original list. This number is usually approximately one-third of the total number of items on the original list. For example, if the original list is 60, then each person will have 20 votes.

4. Working individually, each team member selects the items he or she wants to include by allocating the agreed-upon number of votes.

5. Tabulate everybody's votes. Put a checkmark (or other mark) for each vote an item receives. The items with the most votes are the ones the team as a whole believes are most important.

6. Reduce the long list of items by crossing out the ones with the fewest votes. For example, the team could decide, ahead of time, that unless an idea is supported by at least two team members, it should not be carried forward to the next round of voting.

7. Depending on the number of items deleted from the initial list, and the number of desired items in the final list, the team will likely need to do the voting procedure two or three times (hence the name *Multivoting*). Each round of voting should cut the list approximately in half.

8. To avoid having this as only a mechanical exercise, it's desirable to have discussions in between rounds of voting, where team members can try to convince others of the criticality of their favorite items that may have been weeded out by the team.

9. Ultimately, it may be the responsibility of the leader or manager of the group to decide on the final prioritized list, but with the benefit of the Multivoting input from the entire team.

CHAPTER THREE

Corporate Culture Mentoring

People-Centric Skills

Mentoring; Assessing Corporate Culture

TWO DAYS HAD elapsed since the risk and planning meeting. As Matt entered the Vietnamese restaurant, he saw Meghan sitting at a table waiting for him. The small restaurant was a favorite of Matt's, and he'd chosen it because of the quiet and privacy it afforded. Meghan stood up nervously and they shook hands.

She anxiously asked as they were sitting down, "You aren't going to fire me, are you?"

Matt was going to joke about never firing anyone at his favorite Vietnamese restaurant, but when he looked to see if she was kidding, she seemed worried and tense. Deciding this was no time for his quirky humor, he gently said, "Not at all. Why are you thinking that?"

Meghan took a deep breath and, in apparent relief, smiled. "Well, Lila said you wanted to meet as soon as possible. I know I really botched it during the brainstorming meeting. You warned me before about my needing to establish an environment where the staff is encouraged to contribute and participate. When I went home that night, I rehashed all the stupid things I said, how I said them, and how everybody must hate me now." With a catch in her voice she continued, "I even saw the disappointed look that passed between you and Dalton during my worst meltdown. This isn't an excuse, and I'm embarrassed to mention it, but I just broke up with my boyfriend the night before, and I think it had more of an impact on me than I realized. Not to make excuses!"

Meghan seemed to be running out of words, and Matt decided he'd better reassure her some more. "Meghan, I do want to talk with you about the brainstorming session, but in the context of a broader topic. I first want to reassure you that firing you is the last thing on my mind." Matt observed the calming effect his words were having on her. "Meghan, you're a very valuable member of our team and I think your future here can be very bright."

She replied, "Good! What a relief. I was a bit worried. What is this broader context you mentioned?"

Matt, glad that they seemed to be past Meghan's immediate concerns, responded, "Have you ever had a mentor in your career?"

The question caught her off guard, and she finally stammered, "No, I've never been in a company with a formal mentoring program. However, I have a college friend who told me about mentoring where she works. She said it really helped her; I was very jealous!"

"I understand," Matt replied. "MultiCrown doesn't have a formal mentoring program, either; but that doesn't mean that two people can't establish a mentor–mentee arrangement. This is strictly a volunteer situation on your part, but would you like me to be your mentor? If you decide you would rather not, I would be perfectly fine with it. This type of arrangement is more common when the mentee does not formally report to the mentor, but I think it's okay to have it within a reporting situation as well."

Meghan's face lit up and her eyebrows rose. Even her posture became vibrant. She immediately replied, "Absolutely! I would really appreciate this type of guidance from you."

Nodding his head at Meghan's quick agreement, Matt continued. "Part of my responsibility as a MultiCrown executive is to help develop and encourage future leaders of the company. I have at times selected a few very promising up-and-coming leaders, and offered to be their mentor. It has worked out very well, and I'm still in this informal arrangement with several of our current MultiCrown leaders. Past mentees of mine, in prior companies, have gone on to lead their own audit shops, and one recently became a CFO. We still have informal discussions, even after many years. For me, it's a real source of pride when I can help develop future leaders. It's part of the legacy I want to leave behind.

"To make sure we're on the same page, let me summarize what this will entail. *Mentorship* is a developmental relationship in which a more experienced person, the mentor, helps a less experienced person, the mentee. Mentoring consists of guiding, counseling, and supporting the mentee. The mentor and mentee focus on a broad development goal like becoming a more effective leader, or progressing in an organization. These goals usually cover complex areas of development that are not really found in books. You learn these things through hard experience. It might include advice about networking, strategizing career moves, understanding the unwritten corporate culture, navigating complex organizational interactions, and solving thorny leadership challenges. Does this still make sense to you?"

"It makes perfect sense," she replied. "I think right now I'm struggling with adapting to the MultiCrown way of doing things."

"That's *exactly* the topic I wanted to cover today," Matt declared. "I would like to give you advice so you can succeed at MultiCrown. I know you're going through a lot of changes with a new level of responsibility and a new corporate culture. I want to help you with the transition.

"From my experience, when people fail in a company, it's usually not due to a lack of technical skills, but to gaps in the interpersonal, or *soft* skills—what Dalton calls the *P-C skills*. Mentoring focuses on developing the most *complex* of the P-C skills. You spent your entire career at a company with a very different culture from ours. The confrontational, aggressive style you developed there—to succeed—will *not* work well at MultiCrown."

Matt paused to give Meghan a chance to absorb this. He had mentioned the cultural differences before, but perhaps it had seemed academic to her. Now, after the recent problems during the brainstorming session, in addition to other similar issues, she may be ready to listen. The silence compelled Meghan to say something. "I tend to react to people in the manner I'm used to." In a plaintive tone she continued, "How do I change that?"

Matt softly responded, "Well, you are already *aware* of the problem, and you *want* to change. That already puts you most of the way to resolving the problem. I suggest that for a while, you act as a cultural anthropologist. Step back, observe, and try to understand how others here discuss things, how they handle differences of opinion, and how they react to each other. Find a few people you believe are really successful in our culture and objectively see how they interact. Listening and silence can be great ways to learn. Deliberately dampen your strong emotions for a while, speak softly to others, and put yourself in their shoes. Also, feel free to ask lots of questions of the other auditors about what is expected here. If the auditors, and others, see that you are really trying to learn and understand, they will be very open with their advice. Make yourself pause a moment before replying to what might *seem* to be a challenge. Try to legitimately encourage and help others.

"From my observations, MultiCrown has a friendly, collaborative corporate culture, with a very professional environment. Employees are polite to each other, with very little cursing or shouting. People tend to disagree with each other in a straightforward and constructive manner, and usually with respect. You don't often see very overt cutthroat competition between MultiCrown employees. The employees who get promoted here are generally the ones who can work effectively with others in a collaborative fashion. The focus is on MultiCrown's success. Employees who focus only on themselves, at the expense of their team members, or the Company, have a way of being weeded out. In general, our people have high morale because they are treated respectfully and fairly. In our best divisions, the leaders tend to be participative; that is, they allow their people to provide meaningful input into decisions—they are not dictators.

"Caleb has consistently emphasized that the safety of our employees is extremely important, and we now have a corporate culture where everybody is highly focused on safety. He has also constantly reminded us to behave ethically, obey the rules, improve our operations, keep our promises, and treat each other respectfully. Of course, Caleb is also very tightly focused not only on satisfying our customers, but on *delighting* them. The head of any company or organization greatly determines the corporate culture. Of course, past CEOs have also left their mark on MultiCrown's current culture."

Matt again paused to let Meghan process all this. He was glad to see Meghan nodding slightly at everything he was saying. "Another thing that may be challenging is that you are now at the Director level, which is a very different set of responsibilities than when you were a Manager, with a smaller team of auditors. I noticed that you are so driven to succeed that you sometimes try to micromanage your auditors. We have very capable and experienced people, and you need to give them more rope. Start out believing they know what they are doing and that they will accomplish their tasks. Of course, if anybody is not meeting expectations, you can then gently coach them."

At this, Meghan wryly said, "Just like you're doing with me."

Matt approvingly smiled. "Yes, as I'm doing with you," he said in a direct manner. "Assume that others *want* to do a good job and want to get along with you. You should *help* them to succeed, and that helps *you* to succeed. Something I read early in my career has really stuck with me. People work best when they get seven 'strokes' for every 'kick'—that means seven true and sincere compliments for every one constructive criticism. So, basically, you're observing your people to catch them doing something well, and then you compliment them for it. For example, say something like 'Good planning memo—you really covered all the key risks.' Any criticism, while less frequent, should, as I mentioned, be *constructive*. You don't have to put much heat into it. For example, 'I liked your planning memo, but I noticed you didn't include fraud risks. Why don't you think about this and get back to me with a revised memo?'"

Matt again stopped to gauge Meghan's reaction and she quickly responded, "Yes. I really see how that would be a good way to lead. I am definitely too critical and not encouraging enough."

Matt went on: "Good to hear you self-assessing how you do things. We all need to do that in order to improve. Something else I read in that original article is that in the United States, the actual average is 10 kicks for every stroke—the *complete opposite* of what is best. That was 20 years ago, and I have no clue if the statistics are still true, but my management style is based on this strategy, and it has generally worked well for me. Now, one thing to remember is that this type of coaching does not work for everybody. There have been times when I've come to the conclusion that an employee just didn't get it, and wasn't capable enough to meet expectations. In that case, after trying all the coaching help I could give, I got HR involved and either found a better fit internally within MultiCrown, or asked the employee to leave the company. It's hard, but ultimately this is best for us and for the individual."

Since Meghan was again looking apprehensive, Matt reassured her, "This was not meant as a warning to *you*. I have every confidence you can succeed here. I said it because as our Audit Director, I will need you to be very involved in this type of decision with problematic employees. We have an excellent team, but, as you know, there are two auditors we're struggling with, and we need to decide if they can continue to learn and develop, or if we need to ask them to leave."

"Matt, I understand what you are saying about our two auditors. I have been trying to work with them. I think Laura is learning and growing and I believe she will eventually be fine, but frankly, I'm not sure Adam is going to make it."

"Yes, I have a similar view of Laura and Adam. Let's schedule time this week to specifically discuss both of them. Maybe there is some training we can send them to. I don't want to give up on them yet. But, for now, let's return to our discussion."

Seeing Matt's concerned expression, and after a moment to get reoriented, she nodded and continued. "The corporate culture topic is really interesting to me. I've never had anyone discuss their organization's culture in the way you have. I'm pretty new here, but I have seen some of our operating units that are different from what you described as our corporate culture."

"Meghan, that's a very good observation. We've been talking about Multi-Crown's overall corporate culture, but each division and even each operational unit or organization has its own spin on culture. Or you can call it a *subculture*. We are not a monolithic company. As we talk about 'tone at the top' in internal controls, the same is true with corporate culture. Management can significantly affect the organization's corporate culture. What can be acceptable and expected at one unit can be viewed as unacceptable in another.

"What I told you about MultiCrown's culture is a generality. For instance, in our Plastics Molding Division, morale is not high right now. Their safety statistics are going the wrong way, and it's obvious their customers are becoming more and more dissatisfied with the quality of the products. As you know, we in audit have also had our challenges there. I'm sure you've heard Bill's stories about our recent audit. In a world-class organization, when a unit or division veers off too much from the corporate culture senior management is fostering, there is likely an eventual change in the leadership of the unit."

With a thoughtful expression on her face, Meghan asked, "Matt, are you saying you think Caleb will get rid of Tom Peterson?"

"Meghan, as you can imagine, that is a *very* sensitive topic. I honestly don't know what Caleb might do about the Plastics Molding Division, or if there will be a leadership change there. However, in my opinion, the culture of that division seems to be getting further and further away from the culture Caleb likes. But, this is just my opinion. Meghan; you *definitely* need to treat my comments and observations in strictest confidence. I'm sharing these with you because it's very important, as a leader, that you are also able to read the signs of the subculture in each organization we are auditing. It's part of assessing the tone-at-the-top that's so critical to understanding the control environment.

Also, by understanding the subculture you're working in, you can better navigate the difficult interpersonal landmines. Part of our mentoring sessions in the future might be a discussion of the subculture of the various MultiCrown organizations. The subculture I want you to focus on next is our *own* Internal Audit culture. First, you need to observe how we do things here and understand the type of organization I've been working to develop. Then, both of us can push in the same direction. If you and I aren't in sync, we can confuse the auditors about what behaviors we expect from them. And that can lead to serious morale issues."

Meghan was silent for a long time, and Matt let her think while he ate the Tripe Pho the waitress had just brought him. Meghan started on her Vietnamese Banh Mi sandwich, a much less adventuresome choice than the tripe he was having. After a few more bites of her sandwich, Meghan said, "I really appreciate your patience and your help. I want to do a good job, and I want you to be proud of me. Thank you for your support and your offer to be my mentor. Also, I found your observations about our corporate culture and our various subcultures to be fascinating. Do you think I could call Dalton to get his suggestions as well?"

This question caught Matt by surprise, but after a short moment, he replied, "Sure. We don't want everyone calling Dalton out of the blue, but you are a key member of our audit leadership team, and I'm sure Dalton will be able to help. I'll give him a heads-up that you might call him."

Meghan seemed pleased at his response, but again caught Matt off guard with her overly casual comment. "I heard from Sandra that Dalton recently got divorced."

"Yes . . . it became final a couple of months ago," Matt responded cautiously, not knowing where this was going. He hoped it was not what it seemed. Having Lila, Sandra, *and* Meghan involved with Dalton was a complication he did not want to think about. What was it about Dalton? He has a shaved head and wears snappy three-piece suits, but that can't be it. Matt decided it must be Dalton's confidence.

Meghan abruptly changed the subject and started to ask questions about Vietnamese food. Since Matt felt much more comfortable with that topic, and since his hobby *was* international cuisine, he happily chatted for the rest of the lunch about the influence of both French and Chinese cuisine on Vietnamese dishes.

As they finished their lunch, Matt brought the topic back to business. "Meghan, something else I want you to think about is *you* becoming a mentor to one of our promising managers. You have much to teach a less experienced employee, and it's not too early for you to start establishing your own mentoring arrangement. As you progress in your career, you will then have people you've helped along the way and who might in turn be able to support you. As you think of our auditors, is there anybody you feel is a promising leader you can mentor?

Meghan thought carefully about both the suggestion and the question. "Matt, that's very good advice, but it's a bit scary to mentor somebody. I might mess them up with a bad suggestion. However, I will do my best, especially if you can give me some tips along the way." Noting Matt's affirmative nod and the mumbled "of course," she continued, "I was thinking that Linda has the potential to be a great leader, but we are very different and I hope she would be willing to accept my help. Bill might be another promising leader for us."

"That's exactly what I had hoped you would say. Both are good choices." Matt deliberated for a moment about the possible problem of revealing his thoughts about one Audit Director to another Audit Director, but finally decided that in this case it was for the overall good of the department. It would also give him an insight into how far he could trust Meghan's discretion. He went on, "However, I think Linda is struggling with Jim's management style, and could really use the help of a mentor with a different perspective. Just between us, I'm worried she might leave the Company because of her problems with Jim. I'm also planning to throw some additional challenges her way to further develop her leadership skills, and again, I'm sure she would benefit from your mentorship."

"I'll do it! But, I think I'll wait a month or so before I approach her. First, I want to make sure I have my own head on straight about our corporate culture. I don't want to make her situation worse because I gave her bad advice."

"Great! I appreciate you helping her." Matt replied. "Also, how about if once a month we get away from the office and have an informal lunch so we can do our own mentoring thing? Just ask Lila to schedule a mentoring lunch with me and she'll know what you mean." He was very pleased with the way the conversation had gone. Not only was Meghan willing to accept his mentoring help, but she was on board with helping Linda. As they completed their lunch, Matt thought about how much of a leader's time and effort must focus on the development of the team. Fortunately, this was the part of leading an organization that he really enjoyed.

When they left the restaurant, needing to head in different directions, Meghan, with a very sincere and serious tone said: "Matt, I *really* appreciate your advice and offer to mentor me. I will try very hard to understand our culture. If you see me backsliding, please give me one of your proverbial *kicks!*" With that, they both smiled and went on their respective ways.

People-Centric Skills Highlighted in This Chapter

Mentoring

Mentorship is a developmental relationship in which a more experienced person (mentor) helps a less experienced person (mentee). This relationship is voluntary in nature, with both the mentor and mentee agreeing to it.

Mentoring consists of the mentor guiding, counseling, and supporting the mentee. The mentor and mentee focus on a broad development goal, for example, becoming a more effective leader, or progressing in an organization. These objectives usually cover complex areas of development. These areas might include advice about networking, strategizing career moves, understanding the unwritten corporate culture, navigating complex organizational interactions, and solving thorny leadership challenges.

While mentorship usually takes place outside of a manager–employee relationship, with care by both parties it can also take place if the mentee reports to the mentor, or if they are both in the same organization. However, one downside of the mentee reporting to the mentor is that the mentee would not have an independent advisor in case it is the reporting relationship itself causing problems. Also, the mentee may not want to reveal certain concerns or uncertainties to the supervisor.

Some organizations have formal mentoring programs, where high-potential employees may be matched with an experienced leader for a possible mentoring arrangement. This should still be voluntary for both parties. These relationships may last for a specific period of time (usually a year) in a formal program, at which point the pair may continue in an informal mentoring arrangement. While early in the mentor–mentee relationship the meetings can be fairly regular and scheduled on a periodic basis, the meetings tend to be more situational or goal driven as the relationship develops.

Assessing Corporate Culture

DEFINITION OF CORPORATE CULTURE

The corporate culture is the generally shared and deeply held beliefs that determine how a company's employees interact with each other. In essence, it is the personality of the organization. It is a blend of the common values, ethics, expectations, assumptions, goals, environment, and behaviors that all organizations develop over time. The corporate culture is usually implied and unconsciously understood, not written.

(continued)

Corporate cultures often develop by default, instead of conscious design. The culture grows over time from the behaviors and personalities of the people the company hires, trains, develops, and chooses to promote to higher levels of responsibility. The accepted behaviors are encouraged and rewarded by the organization; therefore, acting according to the expected behaviors further reinforces the culture. Employees who chronically violate the customs of the culture and do not "fit in" usually fail and will likely end up leaving the organization.

An organization's culture may have both negative and positive aspects, and some cultures thrive in the existing environment more than others. In general, a healthy culture is one where the employees are motivated, customers are satisfied, financial and organizational goals are accomplished, laws and regulations are complied with, and the company adapts positively and quickly to changes in the environment. A dysfunctional corporate culture is unlikely to succeed in the long term. Successful corporate cultures need to transform over time as the environment changes, as organizational goals change, as new societal pressures and competitors emerge, and as the national and global culture, at-large, evolves.

In large organizations, it is very likely that the various divisions, departments, and operating units have their own versions of the corporate culture. These are considered subcultures. For the leaders of the overall organization, a challenge is to properly align these subcultures so that they reflect the values and goals of the overall culture.

HOW TO UNDERSTAND THE CORPORATE CULTURE

For employees to be successful, it is critical that they understand the corporate culture. Since an organization's corporate culture is mostly unwritten, there is usually very little documented research that can be performed to learn about the culture. Usually, the best way to learn about the corporate culture is by carefully observing how the employees around you behave, by asking questions, and by engaging in discussions with many people, including employees, former employees, and vendors who work with the organization. Questions about how employees behave and what is viewed as important are the best way to learn about an organization's culture. In essence, act as an unbiased and independent observer. Following are some of the questions that can be asked of oneself and others to begin to understand the corporate culture and subcultures in any organization:

- What are the organization's mission, values, and objectives and are they understood by employees?
- Do employees work mostly independently, or is teamwork and collaboration valued?

- How are decisions made, and how are those decisions communicated to employees?
- Are most decisions made top-down, or is there room for employees at different levels to provide input?
- Is the organization managed in a command-and-control fashion (military style) or is it participative in nature?
- Is this a meeting-driven environment, where decisions are made based on committees?
- How are employees valued, recognized, and rewarded?
- What type of person succeeds and what type of person fails?
- Are there good interactions among departments? Is there a spirit of collaboration, or are there "turf wars"?
- Is there an expectation of being excellent and a stated desire to be best-in-class?
- Is continuous and relentless improvement emphasized?
- Is there a clear expectation that the employees are to follow the rules and comply with laws and regulations?
- Are internal controls expected to be executed properly or is the organization lackadaisical about following the control procedures?
- Is the common management style confrontational and aggressive or collegiate and easygoing in nature?
- What skills and personal attributes does the company value?
- Are training plans developed based on the goals and objectives of the company?
- Is promotion usually from within, or are executives often hired from outside?
- How effectively does the company communicate to its employees?
- Is management generally hands-on or hands-off?
- What is the company's attitude toward technology and modern management practices?
- Are the interactions between employees friendly and collaborative or tense and competitive?
- Are messengers of bad news "shot"? Is it difficult for employees to communicate problems or is this encouraged as a positive way to resolve problems?
- Is consistently working long hours expected for success?
- Does the company promote a family-friendly culture?

CHAPTER FOUR

Managing Conflict with Difficult Executives

People-Centric Skills

Conflict Management; Effective Meetings

T WAS LATE Monday afternoon, and Matt was having a horrendous day. He had been pacing in his office like a caged tiger, not even looking out the window at the Chicago River, as he usually did when troubled or in deep thought. Lila stuck her head in his office, but seeing his mood, decided the budget discussion could wait, and silently vanished without Matt even seeing her.

Matt had just hung up with Tom Peterson, the president of the Plastics Molding Division. Tom was in a rage, raving about the lack of business savvy and incompetence of Bill Dorset, the Audit Manager currently in charge of assessing the internal controls of the Plastics Molding Division, based in Mobile, Alabama.

Matt had chosen Bill to lead this audit because even though he wasn't a very experienced manager, his personality should have been able to work effectively with the erratic and often unreasonable Tom. Bill was a calm, polite, and well-liked manager, and he usually received very high compliments from audit clients. He was very focused on doing what was best for MultiCrown, and he was very good with people. Over the past few weeks, Bill had been apprising him of the emerging audit observations and noting that the relationship between the audit team and Tom was continuing to head south. Probably so as not to disappoint him, Bill had understated the problems, and inadvertently overstated his ability to handle them. As part of his natural leadership style, Matt tried to give his managers space to solve their own problems before he jumped in with recommendations. However, in this audit, the situation seemed to explode so fast that Matt didn't have a chance to even *try* to help.

Matt placed a call to Tom to see if he could understand the issues from his side and work to resolve the conflict. The discussion with Tom confirmed that he was extremely unhappy, but Matt could not get concrete details as to the problem. Tom was obviously upset based on his tone, and it was not something he could get past during this phone call with Matt. What mostly came through was Tom's anger that Bill didn't understand the business problems of the Plastics Molding Division and that he was asking for unreasonable corrective actions. Finally, after letting Tom vent for 20 minutes, Matt offered to head down to Mobile next week to meet with him. He told Tom that he was too important a client to not discuss any serious problem face-to-face. Matt wondered what the long silence from Tom meant, but he was at least somewhat relieved that Tom calmed down a bit and reluctantly agreed to a meeting next week.

After pacing for another 15 minutes, Matt picked up the phone and called Dalton. "Hi, Dalton, do you have a few minutes?"

Dalton replied immediately in his usual cheerful voice: "Sure Matt, what's up?"

"As you know, we briefly discussed the issues that Tom Peterson has had with our audit team and specifically with Bill Dorset," Matt continued. "I just spoke to Tom and he was a raving lunatic. The problem was worse than I expected. I offered to go to Mobile to meet with him to resolve our differences. Can you help us with this one? I must admit, Tom is someone I personally struggle with. I think we both have preconceived notions about each other. I could use your objective perspective on him. It would be great if you could stop by tomorrow morning to meet with Bill and me to strategize our approach. Also, I need to verify that Tom would be okay with this, but could you join us in Mobile next week? Perhaps, if needed, you could facilitate our discussion so we can regain professional relations with Tom. He's a pain, but unfortunately, an *important* pain."

Dalton, in what Matt recognized as his soothing-psychiatrist tone of voice, said, "Of course, I can be there tomorrow. Maybe around 11:00 A.M. to meet with you and Bill? I've other meetings next week, but this is important enough that I can reschedule if Tom is okay with my being there. Tuesday would be best for me, but I'm flexible."

Relieved, Matt responded, "Great, see you tomorrow at 11:00 here. Perhaps after our meeting I can take you to lunch at Ali Baba; I'm in the mood for a gyro and some good hummus. You can tell me how you are progressing with Sandra—or is it Lila this time?" He and Dalton were becoming good friends and he liked to tease him, although the usually unflappable Dalton was hard to tease. He was gratified by the dry cough from Dalton followed by a choked: "Sure thing."

As Dalton hung up the phone, he once again marveled at all the weird international food that Matt ate. Middle Eastern food was fine with him, but sometimes Matt dragged him to places where you couldn't even identify the animal they were eating. He also thought about the project Matt had asked for help on; and in his mind, he searched for the best People-Centric Skills material to use. Conflict management, especially with a high-level executive such as Tom, was always a challenging project.

• • •

It was 11:15 A.M. on Tuesday and Matt was wondering what creative excuse Dalton would use this time for being tardy. Just then Lila escorted a rushed Dalton into his office. She had a frosty look on her face, and Matt thought that Dalton would need to use his best conflict management skills to get on her good side again. Matt suspected that Dalton's outing with Sandra must have really annoyed Lila, but that she would never admit anything so personal. Matt and Lila had a very friendly and professional relationship, and they both had boundaries they would not cross. Matt knew not to delve into Lila's romantic life, but that didn't mean he was uninterested, especially since his Brazil Audit Manager and his consultant could be involved as well.

Dalton immediately exclaimed, "The Eisenhower Expressway was a nightmare! There must have been an accident. Sorry I'm a bit late." Matt made an "it's nothing" wave of his hand and brought the right corner of his lips up in a half-smile, but he had hoped for a more interesting excuse from Dalton. He could certainly have used a bit of amusement today.

Settling in at the conversation nook in the corner of Matt's spacious office Dalton got right down to business. "So, give me the background on Tom

Peterson; the business environment for this Division; any past conflicts; and the current opportunity with Bill and the audit team."

Matt, was somewhat taken aback by Dalton's immediate and uncharacteristic grilling, but pleased to begin the discussion of his problem, or as Dalton termed it, an "opportunity." Matt, a cynical warrior of many years of corporate strife, personally thought that some problems were just *problems.* They might be overcome, but it's hard to view them as positive *opportunities.* Dalton probably believed this as well, but his profession must cause him to speak this way to his clients.

Matt began, "Let me give you a bit of background on Tom to start out. He was a somewhat-successful manager of a plastics molding plant, but three years ago he was promoted to be the president of the entire Plastics Molding Division. Tom is about 55 years old, and he has been with MultiCrown his entire career. He's very old-school and seems to resist all change. Even when he was a plant manager, he always fought back on whatever the auditors suggested. He's not very process oriented, and prefers to deal with each crisis personally. Everything seems to be a fire drill with him. The concept that effective processes and good controls could prevent problems seems to elude him. In his last audit before his promotion, he received a very poor Audit Opinion from our team. I'm sure this still bothers him and might be one of the causes of the current problem, I mean, *opportunity.* Frankly, I tell you this in strictest confidence, I was very disturbed when he was promoted. It seemed to me that MultiCrown was rewarding the wrong type of leader."

"I see. . . . Please tell me a little more about his background and personality," Dalton replied.

With that encouragement, Matt continued, "Tom started out as a Mechanical Engineer, but he doesn't really have a facts-based, rational personality. He's very emotional, mercurial, and resists logical arguments."

Dalton interrupted: "What do you mean by 'mercurial'?" He always pushed back a bit when people used an unfamiliar or uncommon term, making sure it was well-defined. His courses and classes consistently focused on speaking to everyone on the same level and using words that were well-known to everyone. He usually joked with Matt about this, since Matt had an extensive vocabulary and enjoyed using *interesting* words. Matt had once told him he appreciated being reminded to watch his use of unusual words. He really wanted to be clearly understood.

Matt explained: "Well . . . he's moody. You never know when he's going to blow up. His reactions are impossible to predict. He's calm one minute and nuts the next. His language can get pretty rough when he's angry. You always need to 'walk on eggshells' around him. You know, *mercurial*, from the element mercury, which is a shifting liquid with no solid foundation. Probably goes back to the personality of the Roman god, Mercury. Of course, he's smart enough to not be this way if the CEO is around. At those times, he seems to be calm, reasonable, and rational. Sometimes I wonder if he uses his anger and aggression to get his way, especially with our auditors. I know in the past, audit mangers have toned down or removed recommendations in his area because they were afraid of Tom. I covered this with Bill before the audit and told him we needed to be professional, but we can't accept a Division president bullying us into changing our audit report. I assured Bill I'd back him, and that's also why I'm headed to Mobile next week."

Dalton nodded his head and made an appreciative *humm!* when Matt stated that Tom may use anger to get his way. He has seen this type of dubious managerial style before.

After taking a sip of coffee, Matt went on. "Let me cover the business situation with the Plastics Molding Division. This is the most troubled business we have. It had a dominant position in the marketplace in the past, but has lost money for the past four years, and seems to be getting much worse under Tom's leadership. Our major competitor is always one step ahead of us with better products, higher quality, and faster delivery, and is aggressively grabbing our market share. This is not surprising, given Tom's lack of process focus, lack of emphasis on consistent product quality, and the poor employee morale of the Division. Again, this is strictly between us, but I don't understand the patience our CEO seems to have for Tom's lousy performance. I really wanted to have this chance to be totally open with you before Bill joined us. As you can imagine, I can't let Bill know some of what I really think about one of our top executives. However, most of the audit staff knows of our past problems with Tom. He has a bad reputation and is not respected by the auditors."

Reading Matt's mind again, Lila came into the office and asked if she should bring Bill in. Matt, as usual, a bit worried by her apparent psychic powers, mumbled, "Thanks, that would be great."

Bill, a taller-than-average 30-year-old with a slender physique and sandy-blond hair, walked in and with awkward hesitation shook Dalton's hand and nodded to Matt. Dalton noted the uncertain and slightly sweaty handshake. He also remembered that Bill was a new audit manager, promoted about a year previously, and that he was extremely intelligent and well-credentialed. Bill had a Masters of Accounting, an MBA, is a Certified Public Accountant, and was also a Certified Internal Auditor.

Given Bill's high potential, but with only intermediate leadership skills, Matt had been carefully mentoring him, and they had had frequent discussions. Bill knew he was over his head in dealing with Tom, and was very relieved that Matt would be joining him in Mobile next week. He was also glad that Dalton had agreed to help, albeit a bit embarrassed that the assistance was necessary.

After all three were seated, Matt asked Bill, "Why don't you give us a bit of background on the audit issues that led to Tom getting involved in the middle of the audit. I'm sure Dalton will have lots of questions and advice."

Bill, a bit bashful in front of Dalton, began his tale. "Well, we started our audit three weeks ago. We had our typical audit kickoff meeting with division management to explain what we were going to be focused on and to understand how they wanted to be updated on any audit observations we had along the way. I emphasized that nobody liked surprises at the Audit Exit Conference. I explained that we prefer to communicate all issues as they're being developed, with the understanding that some of them might change as we gather more data. We invited Tom to participate in the opening meeting by phone, since he was at another plant at the time, but he never returned my email."

With a pause to catch his breath, Bill continued. "Everything was going fine. We were getting reasonable cooperation, but it was very obvious that with all the job cuts over the past year, they were struggling to do their regular work, let alone answer our questions. We started to see that following the reduced headcount, they had hastily combined duties in many areas and given some of their accounting and IT people much more system access than appropriate. Some roles and functions were discontinued, with nobody picking them up. They really did not seem to consider or understand the impact on processes or controls when they downsized. I did not see any real plans to handle the changes in personnel. We have concluded there's a significant fraud risk and that they don't comply with MultiCrown's SOX requirements. We really think that with some compensating controls, such as enhanced managerial oversight, they could reduce their risks somewhat; but ultimately, they would need to either accept more risk, or make tougher changes."

Bill gathered his thoughts again and continued. "We communicated that our audit report would need to highlight that there are uncovered risks that might cause problems down the line and that, given the size of the Plastics Molding Division, we might have a 'Significant SOX Deficiency,' or worse. The Divisional CFO, while not too happy, seemed to understand this, but the next morning, Tom stormed into the conference room where we were working, and, in front of all the auditors and loud enough for the entire Accounting Department to hear, started to shout that our audit team is 'unprofessional and we don't know what the hell we're doing.' He roared that executive management knows they have reduced staff and has bought off on the fact that some *niceties* needed to be skipped. I tried to explain that we understood this, but also believe that with some minor changes, they could reduce their risk. In any case, I told him our report had to assess the control environment as we found it. He would just not hear it; he continued to rant, and finally stormed out."

Dalton listened intently, organized his thoughts, and commented, "Bill, first off, this is a crappy situation to be in and, trust me, it has happened to me and it happens to every auditor. The key is not to focus on any missteps at this time, but really to focus on what we need to do to repair this relationship; and yes, I do see it as repairable. Now, let's try to understand what the hell is wrong with Tom—excuse my frankness. What do you guys think the root of his problem is? Is it truly your audit observations or is there a longstanding issue here?" Matt elaborated again on what he believed was Tom's deep distrust of Internal Audit, rooted in a critical audit report of three or four years ago, and probably a long history of poor audit opinions even before that.

Dalton continued, "That would make a lot of sense. I've seen this before and, quite frankly, Tom is one of those people that just does not get it. He doesn't understand the role of Internal Audit and what we can do to help the company. Ultimately, it comes down to one thing and one thing only—and, frankly, most conflicts usually come down to this—*lack of trust*. If there is a lack of trust, there will never be a transparent, constructive, and strong relationship." Matt and Bill nodded their heads in agreement. "It does sound like this relationship is really damaged. Matt, do you think we can build some semblance of trust with Tom so that we can be cordial in the future?"

Matt answered thoughtfully, "Tom and I have never had a strong relationship and, since the audit report I previously mentioned, things have continued to go downhill with no end in sight. I see the way he leads and I don't agree with his style, but I also try to put my personal feelings aside. I do think Tom can come around *somewhat* if we're able to show him value, explain what would be in his best interest, and get past his distrust."

Instead of commenting, Dalton interpreted Bill's body language and realized he had something to add. Dalton didn't ask Bill for his comments; instead, he looked expectantly at Bill. On cue, Bill anxiously blurted, "Guys, I know I don't have half as much experience as you do, but I must say I've never run into a ruder, more arrogant jerk in my life! He was personally attacking us! I defer to Matt, obviously, but I've serious doubts that we can repair this relationship."

Dalton appreciated Bill's candor. "I totally understand your point of view. I'll say this: I believe any relationship can be *improved* with time, transparency, and honesty. It's all about cost versus benefit—if we're willing to invest the time, we can repair this relationship—but maybe only partially. However, if the benefit is not worth the cost, we should move on. In this instance, from what I'm hearing, let's see if we can repair this relationship sufficiently so that at least we have a reasonable outcome to this audit.

"Now, it sounds like you took all the right steps from the beginning. You discussed our approach in the kickoff meeting and invited Tom to attend. You made sure the management team was aware of all issues as they were identified. And finally, you made sure we did not state that management was the primary cause of these issues; you were not pointing fingers, you were appropriately focused on the process and control gaps.

"The only step I would have done differently is if Tom didn't feel compelled to attend the audit kickoff meeting, I would have offered to set up a separate meeting for him or, at the very least, sent him an agenda and meeting minutes. Tom wouldn't have been able to say he wasn't in the loop if we took this extra step. We can discuss some Meeting Leading Practices separately to make sure this doesn't happen in the future."

After seeing Bill's nod, Dalton continued, "In order to understand Tom better, I did a bit of research on him, general searches on Google and LinkedIn. I couldn't find him on Facebook—he's probably too old-school. Tom is a University of Alabama graduate and a diehard Tide fan. He appears to be a family man, with a wife and three kids. I bring this up because the more we know about our auditee, the better we can relate to him. Based on his charitable interests, highlighted in LinkedIn, I believe Tom, even with his shortcomings, knows right from wrong and, in general, seems to be a good person. He may not be too capable where interpersonal interactions are concerned, but I think he wants to do the right thing for his business. We should start out with that assumption. We need to move past this deep-rooted distrust he has toward the auditors, and I guess, vice versa. The first step before we can begin any type of conflict resolution is to discuss the basis of all conflict. This, as I said earlier, is lack of trust plus unchecked emotion. Excessive, uncontrolled emotions aggravate most conflicts and prevent any reasonable resolution or rational conversation. Bill, in order to make this work, you'll have to leave your emotions at the door and come into this conversation with an open mind, calm rational thoughts, and super-thick skin. Matt, I also think that it's very important we meet with Tom in person, as you suggested, rather than over the phone, or even worse, email. It's very hard to communicate effectively when you can't see body language—especially, with something as tricky as managing a conflict."

Dalton started to highlight points from his training program, which he knew so well that his advice flowed in long, well-rehearsed sentences. "Let's discuss some basics behind *conflict management* and apply them to our current situation."

"There are basically five styles of conflict management. I wanted to give you both an overview of these five styles in addition to a five-step approach to conflict management. Keep in mind that the five-step approach is applicable to *any* of the styles of conflict management.

"The styles of conflict management are *collaborating, competing, compromising, accommodating,* and *avoiding.* Let's start with the ones that will not likely apply to our situation: *accommodating* and *avoiding.*

"*Accommodating* is one of the most passive conflict resolution styles. With this style, one of the parties gives up what they want so that the *other* party can have what they want. In general, this style is not very appropriate for audit situations since we have to focus on addressing the issues. Our audit issues are too important to give in completely to Tom. In any case, giving in and not communicating a complete and honest audit report is against the professional audit standards.

"*Avoiding* is a style where people tend to accept decisions without questions, avoid confrontation, and delegate difficult decisions and tasks to others. This is a very passive approach that's typically not effective, but it does have its uses. It might be okay for fairly minor issues, although I never liked this style. Again, our problems with Tom are important and have to be faced head-on; this wouldn't be a good strategy for us."

Dalton paused for emphasis before continuing. "Now, I believe we might use any of the other three styles. Which one we use will be determined based on Tom's reaction during our meeting.

"With the *competing* approach, each side in the conflict takes a firm stand. They literally compete with each other for power. This style is often seen as very aggressive and can often lead the other people in the conflict to feel injured or stepped on. In this case, we almost would need to threaten to escalate the issues to the CEO and the Audit Committee. Now, I wanted to bring this strategy up but this is not close to ideal and we should view it as a last-ditch effort. We really should not utilize the *competing* style *unless* Tom takes a very aggressive approach and tries to basically throw out our audit report. I doubt this will happen since it's rare; but, unfortunately we need to be prepared for this. Both sides lose if there is an escalation to the Board. However, it might make sense for Tom to understand the ramifications if we follow this style. Instead, I believe the approach that we'll likely use will be *compromising* combined with *collaborating*, if we can convince Tom it's in his best interest to agree to many of the issues.

"*Collaborating* involves the parties working together to develop a win-win solution. This approach promotes *assertiveness*, rather than *aggressiveness* or *passiveness*. I hate to say this, but with the underlying animosity by Tom, I'm not sure we'll be able to fully collaborate unless he has more flexibility than we anticipate. However, we might be able to utilize some aspects of collaborating with Tom.

"With the *compromising* approach, each person in the conflict gives up something that contributes to the conflict resolution. After we understand what Tom wants, we can possibly give up some wording in the audit report. Perhaps make less important issues into 'verbal recommendations,' and so on. We can compromise *somewhat* on the report tone by selection of words and by giving credit to management on the actions they have taken so far, wherever possible. Again, we really can't compromise on our audit assessments and conclusions without violating professional standards or the expectations of the Audit Committee and Executive Management."

Dalton paused again to allow Matt and Bill to take in what they just heard. Noting their nods and facial expressions, neither had anything to add at this point.

He went on: "Knowing we were going to discuss this, I printed out a page from one of my P-C courses. You can take this with you to help plan for the meeting with Tom." With the three of them looking at the page, Dalton continued, "I like to look at conflict management as a five-step process:"

Conflict Management—Five-Step Process
1. Neutralize.
    a. Eliminate/minimize emotions.
    b. Set the time and place.
2. Create a neutral understanding.
    a. Identify needs for all.
    b. Find common ground.
    c. Strengthen the relationship.
3. Perform root cause analysis.
    a. Examine root causes.
    b. Forge give-and-take.
4. Formulate options.
    a. Brainstorm, don't thunderstorm (generate ideas).
    b. Analyze options.

5. Finalize a solution.
   a. Create criteria.
   b. Build a top-three.
   c. Choose and build.

Dalton then continued, referencing his handout. "Now, gentlemen, I believe we have already figured out and discussed Step One, so let's jump right into Step Two. We need to rebuild this relationship, or at the very least, establish a mutual understanding with Tom. What I would suggest is that when we sit down next week with him, let's spend a few minutes on small-talk; talk about the Crimson Tide or maybe he has something on his desk, shelves, or walls we can identify with and chat about. By finding common ground, it should help the conversation develop positive energy and goodwill. This will start us off on the right foot.

"Then, we dive headfirst into attempting to identify the root causes of the conflict, which is Step Three. In my opinion, for our opening comment on this, we need to say something like: 'Tom, I understand and appreciate your *passion* concerning your division and this audit. I believe we have had some miscommunication here and want to make sure we understand your perspective so we can move forward in a positive way.'"

Matt and Bill were both intrigued by Dalton's word usage, particularly the word *passion*. Dalton explained, "Guys, anyone who has enough emotion to shout about something in the workplace is very passionate. It's a very positive way to acknowledge a negative emotion. We basically spin his shouting as something positive for Tom, and I believe Tom will feel more comfortable talking candidly at this point. Additionally, I think the starting point is acknowledging a miscommunication, regardless of who caused it. This is the best way to not point fingers and hopefully reduce some of the negative emotion. Once Tom is honest about it, and has time to think about why he's so upset, I believe we can identify and work on the root cause of this confrontation."

Bill chimed in, "Dalton, I really like your approach; I think this will begin to build some goodwill and relieve some of the tension between our groups. Then we can talk about the fact that we're all on the same team and we're looking out for the best interest of MultiCrown, which is the most important aspect in this conversation. Maybe we can begin to get some *collaboration* from Tom." Matt and Dalton, pleased with Bill's comments, nodded in agreement.

"Now," Dalton said, "we can continue to focus on Step Three, which is jointly identifying the root causes of the conflict. I don't think we will need a deep examination of what the cause of this conflict is; I think it will come out in the conversation. I also believe in the customer service moniker that the customer is always right; if there are opportunities to apologize for missteps, we must jump at them. Not to necessarily acknowledge we were wrong, but more importantly, acknowledge that we're sorry that Tom saw our intentions in a negative way. This will continue to humanize the audit team and show we're not robots but are out to find the best solutions for MultiCrown. Let's also focus on the nature of our audit observations. It seems to me that this is not a blame game, and that we're really looking out for Tom and his team with these issues that have been identified, correct?"

Both Bill and Matt nodded in agreement and Dalton went on, "If that's the case, we need to stress to Tom that we're protecting him, his team, and MultiCrown, and that these staffing cutbacks came too fast and his team has not adjusted to the additional workload or configured the new roles. Again, we're trying to get more *collaboration*. I've found this is a great way to bring someone around on a solution when they're resisting—not only what is in it for them, but how does it protect them as well. Additionally, we need to make sure that we don't discuss our negative feelings and that we don't use the terms *us* or *them*. We need to continue to stress using *we* and to make sure Tom knows *we* are all on the same side."

After a moment to collect his thoughts, Dalton continued, "From here, Steps Four and Five should be relatively easy, as I've faith that we'll be on the same page as Tom. Instead of focusing on the conflict, we can focus on how we can resolve each of the audit issues and begin to move past this confrontation. We'll ask Tom if he agrees with each issue, focus on the facts, and get his perspective on a resolution. Fact-type conflicts are the easiest conflicts to resolve; we can walk Tom through each audit observation and each step through to the conclusion. We gain consensus by asking for his agreement on each step/fact; when we get to the conclusion, it will be very difficult for him to disagree. We can actively lead him to the right answer. If he vehemently disagrees with an issue, let's understand why and make sure he understands that we have to come to a resolution, whether it's an existing control that we had not considered or known about, or possibly a solution that Tom suggests—our best audit recommendations often come from our auditees. Who know more about their business than they do?"

After this long discourse by Dalton, Matt commented, "I think I understand the various conflict management categories and the different resolution steps. Bill, what do you think?"

Bill replied with some uncertainty, "Well, while Dalton was going over everything it made complete sense. However, I'm not sure I'll be able to keep it all straight if Tom starts screaming at me."

Matt thought about this before replying, "I can see that. I hope if we follow the steps, there won't be a lot of ranting from Tom. Also, with Dalton and me there, maybe he will be more restrained. In any case, I'll start the discussion with Tom, and I won't turn it over to you for the specific audit points until I know Tom is in a frame of mind to listen. If he flies off the handle, I can jump back in; and if that doesn't help, maybe Dalton could facilitate. To me, that would be the last resort. It would be better if we could resolve the conflict ourselves."

Dalton nodded at Matt's comments and murmured, "We also don't want Tom to think we are ganging up on him."

At this reassurance from Matt, Bill expressed confidence that the right plan was in place to speak to Tom next week. After a short coffee-break, Dalton started to discuss further thoughts with Matt and Bill about a few leading practices for effective meetings.

"Guys, I think we should spend a few minutes on how to run meetings. I can suggest a few leading practices that can help alleviate some potential problems in the future."

With support from Matt, Dalton went on: "Let me throw out a couple of ideas in regard to meetings, because these are practical, minor fixes that should alleviate some potential issues in the future. Here are the few simple leading practices that I always recommend, starting with making sure we're using the corporate calendar system to send our meeting invitations well in advance. Make sure people have ample time to prepare, if necessary. Included in the meeting notice should be an agenda. Don't hold meetings without an agenda; it comes across as disorganized. An agenda also lets the attendees know the topics of conversation and any preparation necessary. Even if the agenda is two or three bullets on the topics of conversation, put it together.

"One unique recommendation is never to hand out any paper out during a meeting—if there are handouts, send them out ahead of time or provide them after the meeting. When people are given paper during a meeting, everyone reads it and stops listening. We want everyone engaged during the meeting.

"You should mention that the use of a smart phone to check emails or websites during the meeting should be minimized.

"Also, take formal notes during a meeting. If possible, have one person be the scribe while the others converse; don't rotate this task during the meeting. At the end of the meeting, send the meeting minutes to all attendees so there is no doubt about what was said. Highlight any relevant action items with *who* will do *what*, by *when*.

"Finally, never go over the allotted time for the meeting. Nobody likes staying over, and attendees may lose their focus if the meeting doesn't stay on schedule. They'll be worried about being late for their *next* meeting or task. If you habitually run your meetings over, it will also reflect badly on you, as the organizer. I always like the attendees to leave early; I mention that I've given them back a few minutes of their day. Everyone can appreciate that!"

Matt said, "Dalton, I love your suggested meeting practices and we should implement them immediately. It's a bit more work, but we'll end up with better organized and more effective meetings. Please send me your document with these practices. I'll forward them to the entire staff with instructions that everybody follow them."

Bill chimed in, "I wish I had done this with our audit opening meeting in Mobile. I could have sent Tom the minutes and offered a personal follow-up meeting." Both Dalton and Matt nodded encouragingly at Bill's observation.

Matt wrapped up: "I think we have a pretty thorough approach to our meeting with Tom next week. I'll reach out to him and make sure he's okay with Dalton attending next week, preferably on Tuesday. Let me summarize where we stand: Bill will put together a short meeting agenda and prepare a high-level summary of the audit observations so far. We'll both approach this meeting with open-ended questions; establish a positive rapport; try to understand Tom's concerns; and empathize with his difficult business situation. We'll reduce emotions in the conversation as much as possible, and we'll acknowledge Tom's emotions in a positive light. Bill and I will present the issues in a facts-based impersonal manner and stress we're all on the same team and that we're trying to help the business. Finally, we'll offer to fine-tune the wording on some of the audit observations to alter or remove any hot-button words or phrases, if that would be helpful. We can also see if any of the audit issues are minor enough that we can call them Verbal Observations. I think that's about it."

Bill seemed very relieved and upbeat, commenting, "Thanks for inviting Dalton. It was great to have an outsider's perspective on the situation. I like our approach and feel confident we can move past this issue with Tom next week."

"Bill, that's good to hear," Matt replied. "I've confidence in you, and when we can tap into a resource like Dalton, we would be shortsighted not to. I know this whole issue with Tom has been very painful to you, but I'm sure you'll look back on this event later and realize how much you learned. That's one of the ways of developing your leadership skills. Learn from every event. Sometimes the best lessons come from the most painful situations!"

Bill nodded in appreciation at Matt's mentoring advice and started to leave the office. He said in a heartfelt tone as he got to the door, "Thanks again, Matt!"

. . .

Bill was driving a rental car with Dalton next to him and Matt in back. It had been a difficult trip to Mobile, with a canceled flight and scrambling to find an alternative that would get them to the meeting on time. As it was, they'd probably barely make it. Bill was thinking of all the advice Dalton had given him and was rehearsing in his mind what he would say if Tom started to rant again. He was very glad that Matt would be starting the meeting and setting the stage for a calmer discussion, he hoped.

Matt placed a call to Tom, letting him know that given the change in flights, they might be a few minutes late.

The car pulled up at the Mobile plant, with five minutes to spare, and all three were in a pensive and quiet mood. Matt bemusedly thought how unusual this was, since Dalton was seldom quiet.

As Tom's secretary escorted them into the office, Tom was standing and scowling behind his desk, not too happy to see them. Matt pasted a somewhat forced smile on his face and quickly extended his hand to Tom. "Hi, Tom, it's good to see you again. How have you been? Besides having to deal with the auditors!" Matt's feeble attempt at a little levity seemed to fall flat.

As Tom shrugged his shoulders but remained silent so as not to lose the advantage of his anger, Matt continued, "Tom, do you remember Bill?" and after Tom's curt nod, Matt waved at Dalton, "Let me introduce you to Dalton Zimmer. You might remember, I mentioned him and his work with internal audit at the CEO's Leadership meeting a few weeks ago. We're fortunate to have received Caleb's support for having Dalton involved as a consultant with internal audit. As I'm sure you realize, auditors have all sorts of interpersonal and communication challenges, but we do want to get better."

Tom finally broke his silence, "Well, I'm glad you realize your team has problems and you're trying to fix them." He then turned to Dalton and shook his hand. "Good to meet you, Dalton. I wish *my* division could afford fancy consultants."

Dalton adroitly sidestepped this minefield by cheerfully exclaiming, "Oh, I gave Matt a fantastic price for my work. I'm practically paying *him* for the opportunity to work with the great MultiCrown leaders!"

Matt was worried Dalton was laying it on too thick, but Tom seemed to be amused, so perhaps it was okay. Dalton continued, "Also, please don't think that I'm here because Matt's auditors have serious problems. In my experience, having seen hundreds of audit departments, the MultiCrown audit team is world-class, and it's a sign of their openness, flexibility, and desire to continually improve that Matt invited me to help." Tom nodded sourly, but didn't say anything. He waved them all to the conference table in his office.

As they were sitting down, Matt pointed to the plaque on Tom's wall and excitedly exclaimed, "Did you really win the Southern States BBQ Contest last month? I watch that event on TV every year, but I was traveling to Japan this time. What a fantastic accomplishment. I'm really impressed!" This time, Matt's animated tone was completely genuine. "You may not know this, but cooking is my hobby and I love great BBQ. What was your winning entry?"

Tom seemed to come alive as Dalton and Bill watched the energetic back-and-forth discussion between Matt and Tom. For the next 10 minutes, they were deep into cuts of ribs; ground coffee, cumin, and Habanero chili spice rub; basting techniques; and hickory *plus* pecan-wood smoke. Finally, Tom broke off the discussion and stated in a much better mood, "Well, next time you're in town overnight you'll have to come to my ranch for some good BBQ!"

Matt responded with a genuinely enthusiastic, "I'm really looking forward to it!" They both looked around and realized that Dalton and Bill were just sitting there, with a somewhat baffled look on their faces. This brought the reality of the meeting back to them.

After a moment to refocus, Matt continued in a calm tone, "Look, Tom, I know you're very busy, so how about if we address why we're here. Let me start out by saying that I understand how *passionate* you are about your business, and Bill and I know how hard you are all working to overcome your market challenges. I'm sorry about any miscommunication between you and my team."

While Bill nodded in support of Matt's comment and Tom made an appreciative gesture with his hands, Matt went on, "We know you have had to make brutal cuts in staffing, and given how close you are with your people, this must have been very painful for you. I understand the last thing you wanted was an Internal Audit visit. However, we have found that whenever a business is drastically changing staffing levels, either up *or* down, it really heightens the risk. During periods of rapid change, the internal controls sometimes just don't keep up. When we were discussing the annual audit plan with Caleb and the Audit Committee, they understood this, and wanted Internal Audit to review the processes and controls of the Plastics Molding business as soon as possible to see if we cut staff too fast or too far."

Matt tried to remember all the points and suggestions that Dalton had made to get the discussion off to a good start. He also wanted to subtly bring the CEO and the Audit Committee into the discussion to remind Tom there was high-level attention to this audit, and that he needed to tread carefully with his outbursts. He didn't *want* to use a "big stick" with Tom, but it was fine if Tom understood that Matt *had* a big stick, if needed.

Tom nodded slightly to indicate he was listening, and Matt continued, "The reason we're here is because Bill told me how upset you were with the draft audit observations, and when we talked on the phone last week, I also heard how troubled you were. In a bit, I'll have Bill go through each of the current audit points and we can discuss each of them so we can get your perspective. However, before we do this, let me emphasize that our role is to help *protect* MultiCrown and its leaders, and also to help *improve* the Company and assist it in meeting its goals and objectives. As one of our top executives, we're also trying to protect *you*. Can you imagine what would happen if, because of the Plastic Molding control gaps, MultiCrown doesn't meet our Sarbanes-Oxley compliance requirements? What if our external auditors have to issue a negative audit opinion or what would the Board think if we ended up with a substantial fraud in your division because the segregation-of-duties controls aren't working?"

Tom angrily interjected, "Now, wait a minute! We're not worried about fraud! We have very experienced people and I trust them! I've known most of them for years! The best controls are good employees!"

Matt nodded and calmly explained, "I know you have good employees, but the fraud statistics indicate that the biggest frauds are committed by trusted employees with an opportunity to divert funds."

Dalton jumped in to support Matt, "I've led many fraud investigations, and almost all fraudsters are at the manager-or-above level, and most of them have been long-term, very trusted employees. I know this might not make complete sense, but our highly experienced managers have the most access and, quite frankly, our trust, which gives them the opportunity to commit fraud."

While Tom pursed his lips and displayed a skeptical frown, Matt jumped back in, but in a deliberately softer tone, "The point here is that having good people is important, but so is having effective internal controls. Without sound controls, sometimes even good people are tempted to do bad things. They might be having financial problems, gambling issues, drug addiction, medical expenses, and so on. There are lots of reasons why people commit fraud. Listen, Tom, we're not telling you that we have seen fraud here, only that the controls are now not as strong as they were. They need to be beefed up to prevent possible issues for your business."

At this point, Matt looked over at Bill's worried face and wondered if perhaps Bill suspected fraud. However, it was too late to get sidetracked by asking Bill. He continued, "One last thing—many people think that controls are forced in by the auditors, but as you know, they're not; management designs and executes the controls to keep the processes functioning as desired. We in audit are prohibited by our professional standards to *set* the controls. Our role is to provide an independent assessment and make recommendations of the controls established by management. Management ultimately decides what level of risk to accept and decides what mitigating steps to put in place to manage unacceptable risk. We'll make every effort to recommend efficient and effective controls for you to implement and we might even recommend changes if we think your organization is burdened with *excessive* controls."

At this point Matt stopped to give Tom a chance to comment. Following Dalton's practice, he let the silence encourage Tom to speak. After a few uncomfortable moments, Tom blurted out, "So, if I can accept the risk, why is your audit team bothering me?" He stuck out his lower jaw in a combative manner. *"I accept all our risks!"* he said forcefully, as he glared at Bill. "I knew when we slashed staff, some corners would need to be cut. We don't need your auditors to tell us this."

Matt lowered his voice even more before responding, thinking again of how Dalton kept emphasizing the need to reduce emotions. "Tom, yes, you can accept *some* risks *after* we point them out in our audit report. This way our concerns, *and* your actions, are completely transparent. The Controller, or the CFO, or even the Board might then either accept the risk you want to assume; or, if not, our report would give them an opportunity to get back with you to discuss these risks. However, I would say that any risk that goes outside of your business and can affect our company overall should be discussed with the Controller or CFO or CEO *before* you respond to our report. For example, I know that they'll definitely not accept a risk to our SOX compliance. Everybody's also very sensitive to fraud risks. My recommendation is that we work together so that if we can jointly agree to quick or easy fixes, you can go ahead and start implementing them. This way, in our report, we can state the Plastics Molding Division is already taking action. It will make you, and your team, look more proactive. Anybody can have a miss in the controls, but a good team addresses these as soon as possible in a constructive manner."

At this point Tom got very quiet and after a long silence, and in a calmer manner, blurted, "Matt, you're basically saying that if I fight your report we would look pretty bad. I guess that's probably so, but my hands are also tied. The staffing cuts won't let me *add* the controls back."

Matt responded in an equally calm manner, "Listen, how about if we go through the initial issues with Bill one-by-one, and we can discuss possible fixes or other alternatives. After we work together, there could be some issues that may need more resources, but many could be addressed quickly and with minor changes. At least our audit report may provide a vehicle for your discussion with Caleb and others about staffing. I could also work behind the scenes to suggest a few more resources, if I believe they're essential, and if no other alternative will work. Our desire is not to make you look bad. We really just want to help protect and improve MultiCrown and your division. I'm sure that's what you want as well."

Tom took a deep breath, and in a more positive tone stated, "Okay, let's grab some coffee and go through the issues. I really want to resolve these problems." However, even as he was uttering this positive statement, his head was shaking slightly back-and-forth in an unconscious act of negation. Both Dalton and Matt caught this and exchanged a brief knowing glance. It seemed that even though Tom was stating he wanted to resolve the problems, his body language was indicating otherwise. Apparently, he was still skeptical of the issues highlighted by the auditors.

While they were getting coffee and Tom's back was turned, Bill pasted a relieved smile on his face. He had missed the subtle body language clues from Tom. Matt gave Bill a friendly and reassuring pat on the back, but realized that he might need to get back into the conversation depending on how Tom reacted to the individual issues.

They all sat back down at the table and Bill began, "Tom, please remember we're still in the middle of a number of our audit observations; we need to do more testing, explore compensating controls, and work with your management team to discuss alternative corrective action plans. We won't issue any formal audit observations until we have verified all the facts."

Before he could go on, Tom asked, "What do you guys mean by 'audit observations'? Is this the same as 'audit findings'?"

"This is one of the changes Matt has insisted on," Bill responded. "An 'audit finding' is negative and implies that management had been *hiding* the problem and we *found* it. This is insulting, and not usually the case. An 'audit observation' is a more neutral term."

Tom smiled nastily at this, "It looks like Internal Audit hired a PR firm!" Matt, Dalton, and Bill forced a fake chuckle at this joke/insult.

For the next 40 minutes, Bill quietly and calmly presented five distinct audit observations where it was obvious that the recent staffing cuts and corresponding poor job reassignments contributed to the control deficiencies. Bill, in a very rational and unemotional manner, presented the facts and outlined what he thought were the root causes of each issue. He also described the business impact of each control deficiency. Basically, he was answering the question, "Why should we care about this one?" For the first three audit observations, Bill suggested very helpful and practical steps management could take to mostly fix the deficiencies by shifting some responsibilities within the Accounting and

Information Technology groups and thereby building back appropriate segregation of duties. Tom asked questions, and whenever he seemed to get excited or angry, Bill, remembering Dalton's advice, calmly brought him back into a joint problem-solving mode. For the fourth issue, it was obvious that the problem wasn't a poor control design, but poor execution by the Accounting Supervisor, although Bill didn't specifically blame anybody.

Tom nodded, and, in a sad tone, commented, "Our Accounting Supervisor is going through a serious medical problem with his wife, and his work has really suffered. He's usually pretty good, but he's falling apart. We have had other screw-ups."

Matt quietly interrupted, and in a sympathetic tone said, "We understand. Bill and the audit team will look at our wording to take some of the sting out where we can. However, regardless of our toned-down words, you'll really need to address this."

"Agreed," Tom almost imperceptibly mumbled.

After a moment of silence to let everybody absorb this last point, Bill persevered. "The fifth audit observation is one I'm very worried about. This is the one that has serious Sarbanes-Oxley implications and is probably a 'Significant SOX Deficiency.' Unfortunately, the root cause is the newly implemented inventory management system. When this system was designed, they basically gave all users the same full-system access. Anybody with access to the system can execute *any* transaction in the system, and this is a very serious financial reporting problem. It's also a *huge* fraud risk. We don't see any effective solution that will be easy or inexpensive."

As Bill was explaining the ramifications and root causes of this last observation, Tom's face reddened, his nostrils flared, and his breathing quickened. He looked like he was going to have a heart attack. Matt, Dalton, and Bill looked at each other, wondering what to do next, when Tom in a loud angry voice shouted, "Those damn consultants! We paid them a ton of money to design this inventory system and it has been *nothing* but problems. I'm going to kill them!"

Tom looked like he was going to go right out to his pickup truck to get his shotgun, but Dalton, with his first words in an hour, calmly reflected, "Okay, Tom, I understand your anger. This sounds like a contract management issue. I recommend that after the audit team completes their audit work and carefully documents the problems, you engage MultiCrown's legal team. You may need to sue the implementation consultant if they don't fix the problems. However, I'm sure Legal will recommend you use the audit report to discuss the control issues with them before you mention 'suing' or 'lawyers.' Obviously, it would be best if they agree to fix the system deficiencies without expensive litigation."

At this point, while still agitated, it was clear Tom wasn't angry with the auditors. Tom finally muttered in a petulant tone, "I *hate* calling our lawyers." Dalton, in a commiserating manner, went on, "I get you, but who in their right mind *enjoys* having to call their lawyer?" At this comment, the other three ruefully nodded.

Bill was a bit nervous with Tom's comment about killing consultants, although Dalton, a consultant himself, didn't seem worried. It was a short step to go from killing consultants to killing *auditors*. After an encouraging sign from Matt, Bill started to discuss the audit observations again. "The last issue is an operational one, not a financial observation."

At this, Tom smirked, and in a loud voice exclaimed, "What the *hell* can the auditors teach *us* about operations?"

Bill, with some trepidation, bravely responded, "Well, we have been looking at your spare parts inventory levels across the entire Division. It looks like you have about $950,000 in excess spare parts. We still need to do more work on this, but we calculated you have enough spare parts in some expensive categories to last you 10 or more years of historical usage."

Hearing this, Tom's eyes bulged and he squeaked, "*What?*"

Bill proceeded, "I just got an email from one of my auditors during our break and it looks like almost all of these excess parts are large industrial motors; and they all come from an outfit called 'Falcon Industrial Supplies.' These excess parts are stocked at all the Plastic Molding plants. Most were added in the past 18 months—*after* our last audit."

All four sat back pondering the implications of this bombshell. Matt, the first to recover, commented, "This is now a *potential* fraud investigation. Bill, call the auditor right away and tell him to discretely move on to another area. If it's fraud, we don't want to tip anybody off."

Tom angrily interjected, "Now, wait a minute; let me call our Divisional Production Director and our Director of Procurement. We need to get them both here and explain this right away!"

Matt authoritatively responded, "Tom, we *can't* do that. If this is fraud, and we're not sure if it is, we need to move *very* carefully so as to not compromise an investigation. Let's give the auditors a chance to quietly grab the data so it doesn't disappear. They'll work all night to put this analysis together; if necessary, you and I will jointly call our Chief Legal Counsel. Whether it's fraud or just bad judgment, your division still has a lot of money tied up in needless spare parts."

Tom, with a huge sigh, very uncharacteristically said to Bill, "I'm really sorry about my crack to you about auditing operational issues. You were very right to do this analysis, and I'm glad you brought it out. Matt, go ahead with the investigation; I'll stay out of the way. Since you're heading back to Chicago this afternoon, we'll have a conference call with Bill and his auditor tomorrow morning. We can then decide on the next steps."

Tom stood up and everyone else followed. The meeting was apparently at an end. Tom looked abashed and somber as he commented, "Well, this will be a *hell* of an audit report! But, I now understand y'all are trying to help us. We'll work with you to come up with a good set of action plans. Matt and Dalton, thank you for coming down to discuss these *observations* in person. I really appreciate it. Bill, as soon as you know anything more about the excess motors, please give me a call—even if it's the middle of the night. My secretary will send you an email with my home phone number and my mobile. Sorry to be rushing off, but I'm late for my weekly staff meeting."

Once Matt, Dalton, and Bill were outside the building's front door, Matt turned to Bill and warmly shook his hand. "Good job in there! You really took Dalton's advice to heart. I think even without the fraud issue, Tom was going to be much more cooperative on this audit."

Dalton quickly added, "You both did great! As you were talking, I was mentally ticking off all the points on our conflict resolution steps. I'm going to use this discussion as a case study for my next training program!" Seeing Matt's worried expression he quickly added, "Don't worry. I won't use the MultiCrown name."

Matt turned to Bill and said with emphasis, "*Before* you call Tom tonight, please be sure to call me first. Even if it's 3:00 A.M., call me! I don't want to be blindsided. If, as I suspect, this is fraud, I'll need to give Caleb and the Chairman of the Audit Committee a quick heads-up first thing tomorrow. We will also need to bring in the CFO and Legal right away."

At that, Matt and Dalton got in their rental car for the trip to the airport. Along the way, they did a full debrief of the discussion with Tom.

"Matt, how do you really think everything went?" Dalton asked. After some thought, Matt replied in a satisfied tone, "I don't believe it could have gone much better. We followed the conflict management process, stuck to the facts, maintained our calmness when emotions started to rise, and kept Tom on track. I actually believe we can work with Tom moving forward, and some of the underlying issues we have had with Tom might actually improve. He might still be a very difficult person to work with and might have emotional outbursts that are tough to handle. Unfortunately, we'll probably always have to walk on eggshells around him. What are your thoughts?"

Dalton, focusing on driving, thoughtfully responded, "Matt, I have the same sentiments about Tom. And, I think that while Bill did a great job remembering all we planned on, there's a little more work to do with him and possibly with the team on a few minor tweaks to continue to improve."

Matt made an inquisitive "*hmm?*" as Dalton continued. "Matt, at one point Bill used the term *worried* about one of the findings; I mean *observations*. It's easy to play Monday-morning quarterback but I might have said this is an issue that *could have negative implications. Worried* is an emotionally loaded word and we should try to stay away from it if possible. Bill also mentioned that the inventory system was a 'huge' fraud risk and didn't see any reasonable solution. I might have again used the term *substantial* instead of *huge*, which could be an emotional trigger. I also might not have concluded right away that there is no reasonable solution. Instead, I might have asked Tom if he saw an issue with having no segregation of duties in the inventory system and let him come to the conclusion by himself rather than us stating it as one. Not trying to nitpick, these are a few small tweaks I would suggest. With Matt muttering "makes sense" in agreement, Dalton continued. "Let me add one more suggestion. Now I realize the discussion we had around spare parts turned into a fraud issue, but I believe we initially overused the term *fraud*. *Fraud* is a very emotionally charged word and rightly so. As you know, when people get emotional, rational conversation and communication rarely occur. If we're not 100 percent sure a *fraud* has occurred, I recommend using terms like *misappropriation* or *inconsistency*. What do you think?"

Matt took a bit of convincing but ultimately agreed with Dalton's view on using the term *fraud*.

Dalton continued: "I really liked that you established a personal rapport with Tom right away. That discussion about BBQ and cooking energized you both. If you were pretending, you did a masterful job!"

Matt, in a faked hurt tone replied, "I can't pretend about something as important as cooking! *Of course*, I was interested. Tom winning that BBQ contest really impressed me. I've always thought of Tom as a bit of a jerk, but maybe I need to rethink this. He's obviously good at some things, but I still believe he's in over his head at leading this troubled business."

Dalton uttered a noncommittal "I see."

After a few minutes had elapsed, and to poke at Matt, Dalton, while chuckling, said, "You can't be serious about putting ground coffee on ribs?" Matt remained silent; he wouldn't want to dignify this barbaric question with an answer. Matt had a great sense of humor, but not about something as sacred as cooking.

While Dalton drove another 10 miles, both continued to quietly think about the meeting with Tom. Matt remarked out of the blue, "By the way, good response when Tom commented he could not afford expensive consultants such as you. I'm very glad to hear you'll be paying *us* for the privilege to work with our team!" Matt, realizing that with Dalton focused on driving, he could not see by his expression that he was yanking his chain, quickly said, "I'm just getting even with you about your ground-coffee comment." With that, both chuckled and returned to a companionable silence.

After another 15 minutes, Dalton commented, "You know, between the three of us, I think we gave Tom a much better understanding of the role of Internal Audit and what we're trying to do. I think this understanding will pay considerable dividends for your team in the future."

"I agree," Matt, replied. "I had not realized how little understanding Tom had about what we do. I hope he remembers what we covered. He's had a way of conveniently forgetting conversations."

As they entered the airport rental-car area, Matt again reiterated that he appreciated Dalton's comments and his help in preparing for the meeting. He also agreed with Dalton's suggestions about coaching Bill a bit. Both were happy they had time before their flight boarded to have a drink at the air-port lounge. Matt savored a nice Argentinean Malbec wine with subtle cherry undertones, while Dalton happily gulped a Scotch-on-the-rocks.

People-Centric Skills Highlighted in This Chapter

Conflict Management

Five-Step Approach to Managing Conflicts

1. Neutralize.
   a. **Eliminate/minimize emotions.** Emotions tend to drive irrational behavior and do not promote critical thinking; eliminate or at least minimize emotions and resolve conflicts quicker.
   b. **Set the time and place.** Utilize company norms and try to find a good neutral meeting place.
2. Create a neutral understanding.
   a. **Identify needs for all.** Why are the parties conflicting? What will resolve this conflict?
   b. **Find common ground.** Why are we here, and what are we working toward? Try to find areas of agreement for all parties.

c. **Strengthen the relationship.** Look for common ground and build a relationship with the party in conflict. Working for the good of the organization is an easy way to strengthen the partnership.

3. Perform root cause analysis.

a. **Examine root causes.** What is the real cause of this conflict? Is there an underlying ulterior motive?

b. **Forge give-and-take.** Are there areas in which to acquiesce and apologize in order to move this conflict closer to resolution? Why are we doing this? What are the benefits to both?

4. Formulate options.

a. **Brainstorm, don't thunderstorm (generate ideas).** Begin to move past the conflict and brainstorm ideas to resolve any issues. If both parties come to the conclusion that this must be amicably resolved, this stage will be very productive. If the other party is involved in generating solutions, they most likely will buy into them quicker.

b. **Analyze options.** Are there multiple options to resolving the conflict? Can both parties agree on the facts and brainstorm multiple solutions?

5. Finalize a solution.

a. **Create criteria.** After identifying the root cause, what criteria will be used to measure progress? What needs to be corrected to move forward?

b. **Build a top-three.** What are the best three solutions to resolve our conflict?

c. **Choose and build.** Choose a resolution that works for all; what are the actual steps to resolution?

Five Styles of Conflict Resolution

Note: The preceding process can be used in conjunction with any of the following styles.

COLLABORATING

The parties in conflict promote assertiveness and work together to develop a mutually beneficial solution.

Best used when:

■ There is a high level of trust.

■ Shared ownership of the solutions makes sense—everyone buys in.

■ Parties are flexible and open to varying perspectives.

(continued)

COMPETING

With a competitive approach, the people in conflict take a firm stand. They compete with each other for power. This style is often seen as very aggressive and can cause others in the conflict to feel pained.
Best used when:

- You are very confident you are right and are willing to fight for it.
- Time is limited and a quick decision is necessary.
- Stronger-willed parties try to take advantage of the others.

COMPROMISING

With the compromising approach, each person in the conflict gives up something that contributes to the conflict resolution.
Best used when:

- Both parties and goals are equals.
- Give-and-take on intermediate issues can resolve the conflict to both parties overall.

ACCOMMODATING

The accommodating style is the most passive conflict resolution style. This style is used when one of the parties in conflict gives up what they want so that the other party can have what they want.
Best used when:

- An issue is not as important to you as it is to the other person.
- It is not the right time to fight and you would prefer to simply build creditability for the future.
- The relationship is more important than the fight.

AVOIDING

People who use this style tend to accept decisions without question, avoid confrontation, and delegate difficult decisions and tasks.
Best used when:

- The conflict is small and relationships are more important.
- Emotions are high and others around you can solve the conflict more successfully.
- Looking at the cost/benefit of the issue, it is not worth the fight.

Leading Practices for Meetings

- **Schedule out.** Always have the meetings on the calendar, preferably the calendaring system used by the organization (e.g., Outlook Calendar).

- **Agendas are a must.** Always use an agenda, regardless of length. It shows the meeting organizer is prepared and gives the invitee an idea of why he or she should attend. Allot time by agenda item to assist in staying on track.

- **Stay within the allotted time.** Stay on time so people will more likely attend the meetings in the future.

- **Send the agenda ahead with the meeting notice.** This gives attendees an idea of why they are being invited to the meeting in the first place and any preparation they might need to do.

- **Never hand out any paper out during a meeting.** If there are handouts, send them out ahead of time or after the meeting. When people are given paper during a meeting, everyone stops listening and reads. This practice helps to engage everyone from the onset of the meeting.

- **Smart phones are not smart.** Emphasize that the use of a smartphone to check emails or take calls during the meeting should be avoided or minimized as much as possible.

- **Take formal minutes.** It is very difficult to lead a meeting and take detailed notes; if possible, designate someone to take and record the minutes.

- **Create a meeting summary.** After the meeting, send the summary of the meeting/meeting minutes to all attendees so there is no doubt what everyone heard/agreed on and everyone is aware of all relevant action items.

CHAPTER FIVE

Coaching a Leader to Form a Team

People-Centric Skills

Coaching; Leading Special-purpose Teams; Situational Leadership Model; Facilitator Role; Team Sponsor Role; Team Member Role

MATT HAD HIS feet on his desk, lost in thought, when Lila walked into his office. She had a muffin on a plate and excitedly said, "I brought you a leftover carrot-cake muffin from a meeting up on the twenty-third floor. I figured you were ready for a snack!"

He eagerly stood up and reached for the plate. "Thanks, Lila. How did you know? Are you doing your mind-reading stuff again?" She chuckled and responded, "No, you're *always* up for a muffin!" With that final word, she quickly turned and was already out the door before Matt could even begin to formulate a clever response. Matt, with his feet up on his desk again, relishing a bite of his muffin, dialed Dalton.

He immediately picked up. "Hi, Matt, What's up, buddy!"

"Hi, Dalton. Do you have a few minutes? I want to discuss the next project I think we need help on."

"Great, I'm all ears!" Dalton replied.

"Okay, this is what I'm thinking about. I want us to develop an operational Repair and Maintenance audit program. This is something very few audit departments have tackled. I think we should be able to audit the R&M functions at the plants we visit. MultiCrown spends close to $800 million per year in R&M, so this is a big opportunity for us.

"As you might remember, I have a Lean Six Sigma background, and I'm always looking for opportunities for Audit to recommend ways to reduce variability, minimize waste, and improve productivity. I've taken many plant tours at MultiCrown. After discussing R&M with the operators, I think there are considerable opportunities for improving this area. If we can get our mediocre R&M functions to work at the level of our *most advanced* R&M functions, I think we could save a ton of money!"

Dalton immediately replied, "You know that sounds very intriguing, but can you tell me how the savings would come about and how I can assist? I really don't have much experience with R&M."

Matt didn't need any more encouragement from Dalton and continued in his professorial tone, "Well, a good R&M function reduces capital expenditures because equipment that's well maintained lasts much longer. Also, with proper R&M, critical equipment is less likely to fail and stop production. Well-maintained equipment also helps meet quality expectations. Finally, it's usually much more cost-effective to maintain equipment in good shape than to repair it once broken.

"There is little an auditor can tell a maintenance engineer on how to technically restore equipment. That is beyond most auditors' skills. However, we *can* assess and test the R&M *process*. Auditors are experts at processes, and can recognize what it takes to capably execute a function. With some research, auditors should be able to recommend improvements that would enhance the efficiency and effectiveness of our R&M processes."

Matt paused after this long discourse to see if Dalton was awake. Dalton signaled his attention. "Yes . . . I can see how important the R&M function is and what audit could theoretically do to recommend improvements."

Matt continued, "When I was at AeroDiscs Inc., I launched an effort to create an R&M audit discipline. This eventually became a very well-established and valuable audit effort, and I'd like to recreate this success at MultiCrown. We invited the best R&M engineers in the Company to join several of my audit managers to form a special project team to create an R&M audit program. They also created a full-fledged guide the auditors could use as a reference to execute this program.

"Forming this type of team here is where we need your help. My team back then really struggled. The engineers looked at the world very differently than my audit managers. They couldn't agree on the mission or how to go about doing their task. They fought like cats and dogs, and it took many meetings over eight months for them to come together as a team and create what I'd requested. I now know quite a bit more about team dynamics, and I understand some of the things that went wrong with that team. I'm sorry to have to say, I was not clear in my expectations, and didn't provide team facilitation or required interim deliverables. I also didn't monitor their progress appropriately.

"What I'd like from you is facilitation help in launching the team and then to meet with them along the way to make sure they are going in a good direction. Teach them the stages of team development and help them progress as quickly as possible. Help us agree on the team mission, help create the ground rules for the team, establish a structured methodology for them to use, agree on the frequency and format of the progress reports, establish how team decisions would be made, and so on. I'm sure you know all the things a project team needs to do in order to be successful and efficient." Matt deliberately stopped talking.

On cue, Dalton, commented, "Sure, great idea! I've a good set of People-Centric skills for team dynamics and I've facilitated dozens of project teams. How do you want to proceed and when do we start?"

Matt excitedly continued, "I've already started. I received support from Caleb. Then I called three divisional presidents and conveyed that I wanted to partner with them on this effort. I gave them an edited sample of results from my prior company to really explain what this was about and convince them of the value. Even Tom Peterson, after some grousing and grumbling, agreed to provide his best maintenance engineer to join our team."

Matt's tone got more serious and his voice deepened, "This is an aside, but the $950,000 excess spare-parts issue down in Mobile turned out to be a fraud as we suspected when we were there. We are still gathering evidence for the Alabama District Attorney. Unfortunately, this is now protected under attorney–client privilege and our lawyers don't want me discussing this, but someday I'll be able to share the gory details with you. However, I do think this incident has convinced Tom to partner more with us and contributed to his agreeing to lend us an engineer. Frankly, I'm not sure Tom's career will survive given the significant control weaknesses that permitted this fraud, but he's survived other fiascoes before."

Trying to quickly move past his last comment, Matt continued, "Besides the three maintenance engineers, I thought I'd assign three audit managers to the team. I'll be the team sponsor or team champion, and, given my past experience with R&M audits, I'll also be a technical resource to the team. I hope wearing three hats won't confuse things too much for the team. I'd be the boss, the team sponsor, *and* a technical consultant. Do you think this will be a problem?"

Dalton mulled this over and replied, "It's a bit more convoluted than usual, but if we explain it all up-front, it should be fine. What audit managers were you thinking of? Sandra?" Dalton's voice went up an octave at this point, and Matt grinned into his phone.

"Yes, she'll represent the international point of view for us, but don't get too excited—after the kickoff meeting, she'll mostly participate over videoconference. Trips back and forth to Brazil are expensive. I plan to also include Meghan, our Financial/Operational Audit Director. I had a mentoring discussion with her, and want to see if she's getting better at soliciting and accepting constructive input from others. I also asked her if *she* would be willing to mentor Linda Hernandez, and she agreed."

After sipping from his coffee mug, Matt went on. "I'm making Linda, our IT Audit Manager, the team leader for this project. She has a lot of leadership potential and I see this as a developmental assignment. I hope it won't be a problem that Meghan is actually higher up organizationally that Linda. What do you think?"

Dalton thoughtfully replied, "It may cause some problems for Meghan if Linda is the team leader, but really, Meghan needs to improve her P-C skills to the point that she can gracefully accept this type of situation. It will give us a chance to work on developing Meghan as well as Linda." Knowing that Matt liked to subtly tease him about Sandra, he continued in a deliberately deadpan tone of voice. "Sandra should fit in really well, and she seems to like Linda. She's a bit leery of Meghan, but the entire experience should be good for all three of them. If you could only add Lila, it would be a perfect team."

With a smile, Matt chose to ignore this comment and went on. "How about if we schedule the kickoff meeting for the team in a couple of weeks? We can do an initial three-day meeting to make the travel costs worthwhile. I really prefer a short, intense team effort that will give us results faster, rather than one that's drawn out over many months. That's another reason why I want the team dynamics to be perfect for this one.

"Let me contact the six potential team members, send a formal invitation, and a rough agenda for the three days. We can use our conference room. If we all agree on timing, perhaps you can meet with Linda and me in a few days to strategize the kickoff meeting. Okay?"

"That sounds perfect," Dalton replied. "Let me also do a bit of research on R&M practices so I'm well-versed at the team meetings."

Dalton was ready to hang up the phone, when Matt unexpectedly continued talking. "Listen, I think you and I may need to do *two* different sessions with Linda. One session to help her prepare to launch the cross-functional team, but I think first we should do a coaching session with her on basic team leadership skills. As you know, leading a special-purpose team is quite different from being the supervisor of a group. In modern organizations, being able to work effectively in cross-functional teams is a very important skill. I really want to support her as much as possible to make sure she succeeds in this project."

"That makes sense," Dalton replied. "I've some good material on team leadership skills for special-purpose teams. We can work with Linda for a couple of hours. Of course, it takes many years of getting into trouble and pulling out of it before one really masters leadership skills, but we can give her some important basics. As we work with her on this team, you and I can reinforce these basic skills."

"Great!" Matt enthusiastically replied. "Let me schedule some time for us to meet with Linda in the next week or so. Fortunately, she's doing an in-town audit this month and should be able to break away for a few hours here-and-there to meet with us."

After hanging up the phone, Matt carried the plate to the window, where he slowly finished his carrot muffin as he pensively looked down at the passing boats below.

• • •

Several days had gone by since Dalton's phone conversation with Matt. Dalton was speeding through traffic as much as reasonably possible during Chicago's rush hour. Even after numerous visits to the MultiCrown headquarters, he still struggled with the traffic and getting there on time. There is always too much to do and too little time when you're running your own company. Dalton loved the relationship he had developed with Matt and MultiCrown, but now he was in need of an administrative assistant to help continue to push his practice forward. These issues, combined with the divorce and his desperate need to see his young children, had added to Dalton's level of stress. He was greatly looking forward to the coming weekend, since the kids would be spending it with him.

He probably needed them as much as they needed him. Now, if he could only do something about this infernal traffic. . . .

While waiting for Dalton to arrive so they could plan the launch of the R&M/Audit team, Matt and Linda were quietly talking in his office. As Matt looked at Linda's expressive face, he was glad to see she was excited about the new project. He had been worried about Linda, normally very vivacious, friendly, and outgoing. However, her personality clashed so much with her direct boss, Jim Franklin, that Matt was afraid Audit might lose her. Given Linda's potential, that would be a big loss for the audit team. One of the reasons Matt chose Linda to lead the R&M/Audit team was to get her away from her boss, Jim, and give her a very visible, important project of her own.

After a contemplative silence, Matt commented in an encouraging tone, "You know, Linda, this team will be a great developmental opportunity for you. I have very high regard for your abilities, and I really expect you to grow into a wonderful leader for the Internal Audit department *and* for MultiCrown. This team effort, being apart from IT, will give you invaluable experience dealing with a different set of professionals in a cross-functional project. Also, there are many MultiCrown executives watching this effort, so a success here will be great for your reputation."

Linda smiled a bit apprehensively. "Thank you! I really appreciate the opportunity. I want to make sure not to disappoint you. I do have to admit I'm somewhat nervous. I don't know much about R&M, have never worked with engineers, nor have much experience with development teams. I'll really need your help and Dalton's advice."

Matt immediately and positively replied, "You've got it! As you know, I've done this type of project in the past, and I can help you on this one. Also, Dalton will facilitate the initial team meetings to make sure you're off to a good start. He's really an expert at this, and you'll be in great hands. We both want to give you plenty of *coaching* assistance to help you succeed."

She looked somewhat reassured, but still worried. "I'm not sure what you mean by *coaching*. I view a coach as something a sports team would have."

"Well, that's about right," Matt explained. "A coach instructs a person to help achieve a specific goal or to perfect a skill. For example, in tennis, a coach might focus on teaching the mechanics of the backhand stroke. He might give exercises to the player to help improve power and accuracy. In a business environment, you may see a coach helping others to improve a business skill. No matter what the area of focus, a coach specializes on improving a few areas at a time. In our case, Dalton, who is an expert on teams, will *coach* you on what you'll need to know to develop or improve your team leadership skills."

Linda thought about this. "Makes sense; I guess, when I teach new auditors how to evaluate computer system access or how to prepare workpapers, I'm acting as a coach."

"Exactly," Matt responded. "Teaching others how to improve their skills is one of the most important roles for supervisors, managers, or even employees with specific expertise. The more skilled our employees become, the more successful they'll be. This will help them, you, me, Internal Audit, and MultiCrown. When you're acting as a coach, it's very important that the people you're coaching trust you to do what's best for them. You'll need to be respectful and constructive in your approach, which, of course, you always are. If people think we have ulterior motives for coaching them, or if we make them feel stupid or inadequate, they'll turn off and not learn."

Linda thought about this and hesitantly commented, "Yes, I had a 'coach' who recently made me feel like an idiot for not knowing how to do a risk analysis on an old legacy system I wasn't familiar with. He seemed more interested in making himself seem superior than in helping me."

Matt strongly suspected who Linda was referring to and was about to probe, when Dalton swept into the office like a cyclone, with a harried-looking Lila trailing behind him. Lila preferred the old-fashioned practice of politely escorting guests to Matt's office and making sure Matt was ready for them, but Dalton's energy and disregard for some conventions often stymied her. However, this exuberance was also one of the things she really liked about Dalton. With a rueful expression on her face, she asked, "Dalton, would you like some coffee? Matt and Linda, do you need refills?"

With a simultaneous "Thanks, Lila!" from all, she went off to get their coffees. Without further ceremony or apology for being a few minutes late, Dalton sat down.

Matt immediately began. "I've given both of you the background for the kick-off meeting in two weeks, so I think we can jump right in. Dalton, as we discussed earlier, today we need your coaching skills to give Linda some basic team leadership suggestions. This can set the foundation for a follow-up session to discuss the more specific aspects of launching a successful team. At that time, you can give us a brief overview of the key team dynamic factors we'll need to focus on."

Dalton observed Linda's body language. Her posture was very upright and she continued to bite her lip; this was her telltale sign of nervous apprehension.

"Okay, Linda, relax. This shouldn't be painful at all," Dalton started with a chuckle to put Linda at ease.

Linda was quite surprised at this comment since she did not realize her non-verbal expressions gave away her feelings so easily. "As I explained to Matt a few days ago, the team leadership basics we're covering won't make you an expert, but should really help you keep some things in mind as you lead this team."

While still appearing a bit nervous, Linda enthusiastically commented: "Dalton, I'm very excited by this opportunity Matt's giving me, and I really appreciate your help in getting me prepared."

"Great! Let's get started. Something to understand right off the bat is that leading a special-purpose team is different from being the supervisor or the manager of a department. If you're the *manager of a department*, your employees formally report *organizationally* to you. You control their pay, raises, assignments, and promotions. You, as the manager, would also be responsible for making the key decisions and accountable for the results. However, a good manager solicits ideas and listens to employees. Does this make sense?"

"Sure, Dalton." Linda glanced at Matt and went on, "You described some of the responsibilities Matt has for leading the Internal Audit department. Of course, he does much more in terms of setting and driving our vision, representing the Audit department with other organizations, providing resources, and many other things."

Matt nodded in acknowledgment of Linda's comments, but didn't want to break Dalton's train of thought and remained quiet.

"Yes," Dalton remarked, "that type of manager or leader role is what most people in organizations are used to. However, leading a *special-purpose* team is something different.

"A special team is one that is formed to accomplish a specific or *special* objective. After the team accomplishes its goal, it's disbanded. These project teams might be launched to improve quality in a process, solve a significant problem, or perhaps develop a new product or process. In our case, Matt is forming the team to create a new product for Internal Audit—basically, to develop a new operational audit discipline to review and improve the R&M functions at MultiCrown. Very often, the team members in special teams come from different organizations and they don't usually report *formally* to the team leader. I see more and more organizations using these types of cross-functional special teams to tackle important issues."

Linda mulled this over before replying: "Okay, I understand why leading the *special* team to develop an R&M audit discipline is different from leading an audit department, but if the members of this team don't report to me, then how do I get them to do what I need them to do to meet our objectives?"

Dalton could tell by Linda's furrowed forehead that she was troubled or confused. "That's exactly the point," Dalton explained. "You don't coerce them to do what you want. The team members work *collaboratively* to accomplish a goal that they've all bought into. In this case, part of Matt's job as the team sponsor is to provide the direction and objectives for the team. He'll recruit team members from the R&M organization by convincing the presidents of the various divisions and the R&M engineers themselves that the team objective is valuable and worthwhile for MultiCrown. If Matt can convince them, then the R&M engineers and the auditors on the team will in essence direct *themselves* to accomplish the objectives. However, your role as the team leader is essential for the team to accomplish its goals."

While Dalton paused to take a breath, Matt quickly jumped in, "I already discussed this with our CEO and three of our division presidents, and they agreed to support the project. We have three R&M engineers assigned, and we'll add three members of the Audit group to form this special cross-functional development team."

"Let's cover the responsibilities of the team leader and you can ask questions along the way," Dalton continued. "A key objective of the leader is to encourage the rest of the team to have a strong focus on successfully reaching the team objectives. You achieve this by working *within* the team rather than directing it as a manager from above. An important factor is that the leader needs to be respected by the team members, who will then be willing to work together with him or her. The leader should also be enthusiastic and focused on accomplishing the team mission. You'll need to encourage your team members to keep going until the mission is done. You'll also help the team stay organized so that the necessary activities are carried out on time. In addition, you, as the team leader, *don't* make the team decisions. The team *as a whole* makes the decisions."

When Linda nodded, Dalton kept on going. "Let me expand on all of these points. As you can see, having a very clear team mission that everybody fully understands and supports is essential. This sounds like a no-brainer, but I've been surprised with some teams where the team members had different views of the objectives. These teams fractured as each team member worked to accomplish his own goals at the expense of the overall objectives. I'll cover this in much greater detail with you and the full team later on, but as the team leader, you'll lead the team to write a Team Mission Statement. By all of you working together on this, and specifically detailing the key aspects and deliverables of the team, you'll help ensure everybody understands the team goals."

At this point, Linda interrupted. "Dalton, do we *really* need to get so formal as to create a *written* mission statement? It seems that if we discuss it and all agree to the team objectives, this would be enough. We're professionals."

He replied, "You know, everybody may verbally agree on the team objectives, but people have a way of forgetting what they agreed to. As the months go by, the team members may remember the version of the mission that *they* prefer rather than the one everybody agreed to. By writing it down in a formal manner, it's much easier to keep everybody focused and helps avoid some misunderstandings and conflicts. It really is worth the time and effort. A good idea, especially in early team meetings, is to start the meeting by everybody spending a minute or two reviewing the Team Mission Statement. As the team progresses, you will know when everybody is on the same page and you can scale back on this. Sometimes, even many months later, you may have a team disagreement and you will need to pull out the mission statement again. Also, the mission statement is a good way to communicate with other people outside your team so they understand what you are working on, and why. In addition, it is the formal contract with the team sponsor to make sure there are no discrepancies in understanding the objectives. Does this make sense?"

She quietly commented, "I see; thank you for explaining it."

Dalton deliberately paused to see if Linda really understood. Sensing she was expected to comment, Linda said, "So, going back to my original concern about how to get team members to do something, what you're basically saying is that if everybody understands the mission clearly, *and* if they really buy into the mission, they'll be *self-motivated* to do what is needed without my *ordering* them to do so, which is a good thing, since I don't have the authority to *order* them to do anything."

Matt had been letting Dalton carry most of the discussion so far, but at this time, he quietly commented, "Even with leading an organization or department you'll find that managing professionals is often about getting them to buy into the goals. Good employees should be very motivated and self-directed once the objectives are clear. For example, how often do I need to give you an *order* to specifically do something? When I think we have a risk in an Information Technology area, we discuss it and we might jointly agree we need to do an audit of some kind. Alternatively, you might be the one who believes we've got a risk and come to me; and we again might agree to move forward with a specific audit. You then go back to your office, think about it, maybe do some research, and propose a specific action plan to me. We then would work together on your proposed plan until we have a clear path forward. As leaders, we want to develop and encourage our employees to be self-motivated. There are different leadership styles, but the last thing I personally would want to do is to have to order detailed instructions for professionals as if they were unmotivated and unskilled robots. When leading special teams, you will need to take this concept even further, since as you pointed out, you have no direct authority over the team members. They will *need* to be self-motivated."

Linda seemed to debate with herself whether to say something, but finally blurted, "I agree that you rarely give me detailed orders on how to do something. You usually present me with what we need to accomplish and why, and then you trust me to develop an approach. I really appreciate this style. You treat me as a professional. However, Jim often gives me detailed orders telling me how to do things. . . ." At this point, Linda appeared to be uncomfortable and stopped talking, realizing that criticizing her direct boss might not be appropriate, especially in front of Dalton.

Matt carefully said, "I know that Jim's management style is a more *directive* style than a *delegating* style. Depending on the type of employees you're managing and their roles, his style *may* be appropriate. However, I've found that for highly skilled and motivated professionals such as our auditors, a delegating or participative style works best. I suggest you read about something called a Situational Leadership model. We have a copy of the book in our audit library. The basic premise of this model, also called the Hersey-Blanchard model, is that the key to effective leadership is to focus on the attributes and styles of the *followers.* In essence, if the followers are capable and motivated, then the leader should have a *delegating* style. Let's have this discussion about you, Jim, and the Leadership Model offline so we don't take Dalton's time. Please work with Lila to schedule time for this."

"Okay, then," Dalton went on, "one of the things you will find is that some of your team members will often meander in their comments, and might talk about things that are irrelevant to the mission. As the team leader you can, of course, use the Team Mission Statement to *gently* help refocus everybody on what you're all supposed to accomplish. You'll need to have good judgment about this; sometimes thinking outside the box to come up with the best solutions means that the discussions just *seem* to veer off from the team objectives. As you get to know your team members, you'll have a sense for when somebody is being creative versus really going in a different direction.

"Another possible technique for keeping the team focused on your mission is to maintain an Idea Parking Lot. Basically, you create a document labeled 'Parking Lot.' When somebody comes up with an unrelated, but potentially valuable suggestion, you offer to add it to the Parking Lot for further discussions later on. At a future meeting, you can set aside a specific time to cover the Parking Lot items exclusively. An advantage of using a Parking Lot is that your team members won't feel insulted if you need to cut them off to refocus the team. You're signaling that you're not *ignoring* their input;

you're only setting it aside until it can be fully explored at a better time. Of course, you will need to explain this tool to the team since it might not be obvious how it works."

"Let's talk a bit about team decisions," Dalton continued. "In a department such as Internal Audit, the leader is accountable for the critical decisions. The leader, if a good one, will, of course, get input from others; but, ultimately, it's the leader's job to make the tough decisions. If it's the wrong decision, he or she will need to live with the consequences. In a special team, as I mentioned earlier, this is not the case. The team leader does *not* make the decisions and is not accountable *individually* for the outcome of the decisions. *All* the team members, *including* the team leader, discuss the facts and considerations of the decision and make the decision together. The leader has no more say than any other team member. You're all equal in this. However, if the decision is really important, and significantly affects the team mission or the project timing, the full team would then *recommend* an action or a decision by the team sponsor, in this case, Matt. He would then make the decision, not the team. One of the items I'll cover with the full team during our first meeting is a discussion of how team decisions are to be made."

"It seems the team won't move very fast," Linda remarked, "if we need to stop and all agree on every decision."

"You'll be surprised how fast a team can get at making decisions," Dalton replied. "I'll cover this later on at our follow-up meeting, but teams go through different stages of development, and as the team gets more advanced, joint decisions can be made very smoothly and quickly. Even if team members have different opinions, and they *should* have different opinions, these various views will be carefully considered by the team and the members will come up with a best decision for the team as a whole."

Linda still seemed somewhat unconvinced, but Dalton reassured her. "I'll help you with the first couple of meetings, and you'll see how teams make consensus decisions. The main point here is that you shouldn't try to make the team decisions by yourself. The rest of the team will likely resent this and you might set an antagonistic tone that would be hard to recover from."

"Sounds good; I trust you," Linda said, with a shaky smile.

"Great! Let's move on to the next point. I mentioned earlier that the team leader should organize the logistics and activities of the team. So, for example, the team as a whole decides how often to meet and for how long, but the team leader is the one who actually schedules the meetings by sending out calendar notices, books the room, or sets up the conference call details. The team might decide as a whole what individual assignments will be presented and discussed at the next meeting, but the team leader will prepare the agenda with these items and estimate the time slots required. The team leader will keep the team on track to cover the agenda items.

Linda mulled Dalton's suggestions for several long moments, but Dalton gave her space to absorb the advice and waited for her to comment. Finally she said, "Okay, that's logical; anything else?"

Matt, who had been quiet during Dalton's last comments, spoke up: "There are a couple of additional points we need to discuss. An important aspect of the team leader role is to keep the team sponsor informed of the team's progress. Since, in this case, I'm the team sponsor, we need to decide in what manner and how often you'll keep me up to date."

Linda replied, "How about if I talk with you after every meeting?"

"You know, I probably don't need to look over your shoulder *that* much," Matt responded. "How about this: After every meeting, you can send me the team minutes, with a cover email where you can briefly let me know how you believe the team is progressing and highlighting any problems or concerns. With the email, feel free to ask for a more detailed discussion if there's anything you particularly want to talk about. Then, once a month, let's schedule a full-fledged meeting where we can discuss the team progress in depth. In your emails to me, please copy Dalton so he can suggest anything along the way. You also may want to meet with me just before I am supposed to approve a project milestone; that way I can be fully prepared to do so."

"Good! I'll do it that way," Linda quickly replied.

Matt went on in a pleased tone, "There is another thing. Part of my job as the team sponsor is to get the team the resources needed to accomplish your mission. Also, I will help break down any barriers the team encounters. Your role as the team leader is to act as the main interface between the full team and me. So, if the team needs anything or encounters resistance, please let me know right away."

Linda, with some hesitancy said, "I understand the *resistance* part; I guess any auditor would. But, can you give me an example of the resources you envision? I don't want to ask for too much; I know our department has a budget."

Matt chuckled, "Sure. I appreciate your keeping our budget in mind. But, let's say you want to get the team physically together at a certain point, and you need travel funds to pay for the trips. By the way, we probably should also pick up the travel costs for the maintenance engineers on the team. In that case, you come to me and explain why you need to meet; and if I agree, I'll support you with the funding. Or, let's say you need to bring in an outside R&M consultant to help the team with some aspect of your mission. You can then discuss it with me, and if the request is reasonable, and if we don't have an internal expert, I would likely support the request. I can *always* take it out of our consulting budget and pay Dalton a bit less." As Matt said this he glanced at Dalton and saw that he picked up on the kidding tone. He was glad that the relationship with Dalton now had progressed to a point where he could yank his chain about something as important as consulting fees.

"Thank you," Linda said, apparently oblivious to the byplay between Matt and Dalton. "It's good to know we can get what we need to succeed. However, I promise we'll be careful in what we ask to make sure it's really needed."

After a nod acknowledging Linda's restraint, Matt continued with utmost seriousness, "Linda, there is one more thing a team leader, and actually *any* leader needs to be, and that is *trustworthy*. Having your team's trust is absolutely essential to success. However, I am not sure this is really a skill that can be taught. It's an innate part of your character and part of your values. I would advise a few things you *can* do. If you commit to doing something by a certain date, make sure you do it. This is part of being trustworthy. Your team needs to know they can depend on you to do your part as you promised. If you start to miss your commitments, then the team will take their guidance from you. Soon, nothing will get done on time.

"Also, don't criticize team members behind their back. This might get back to the person you are discussing and it will destroy trust. Also, the person you are talking to will likely think that sometime in the future you might speak behind *her* back. If you have a problem with any team members, tackle it directly and honestly with them. They need to know that you'll treat them fairly, give them credit for their contributions, deal with them respectfully, and in general have their best interests at heart. If you fail at these, you will lose their trust. In that case the team will fail.

"Part of the reason I chose you to be the team leader is that I really trust you and I believe the auditors trust you. However, I wanted to give you this bit of caution, because it's easy to make a mistake and loose the trust of others."

Linda, reacting emotionally to Matt's strong approval, finally choked out, "Thank you for your trust! I treat people the way I want to be treated. I *won't* let you down."

Dalton, after a brief silence to see if Linda would say anything else, summarized the things Matt had said to reemphasize their criticality. "The points Matt brought up are really important aspects of the team leader role. You'll be the main point of contact between the team and the sponsor, so it's up to you to keep Matt informed on the team progress; also, you're the one who would ask Matt for assistance with the team. What Matt said about trust is absolutely true. I also want to make sure you ask me, as the team facilitator, for any help you need along the way."

At this Linda commented, "You know, Dalton, I'm not sure I fully understand the team facilitator role and how it fits in with the team leader role and even with the full team. I could guess, but it would help me if you could explain it to me."

At this comment, Dalton, with a chagrined expression on his face said, "You know, I do so much facilitation for teams that I sometimes take it for granted people know what this is. You're absolutely right. It's *much* better to be very clear in all our roles."

"In essence, facilitators are skilled communicators who are knowledgeable about group processes and experts at interpersonal interactions. These are basically People-Centric Skills. The facilitator assists the team in achieving its goals by guiding the team in team processes. The facilitator should be an *objective and impartial* person who is detached from the area being improved. This allows the facilitator to remain active in team processes but neutral on content. So, I don't need to know much about the R&M discipline, since I won't be making any suggestions on this area. You, as the team leader, and all the team members, will focus on content—that is, R&M and auditing—and I will focus on how you interact with each other. I'm the one who also would suggest the techniques you might use to accomplish your mission. For example, I might help the team with a process to creatively generate ideas. I'll also help the team draft the mission statement. Or, I may suggest team guidelines or ground rules for you to use."

Linda absorbed Dalton's comments before replying. "Will you be a *member* of the team? How about participating in our decision making?"

"Good questions," Dalton retorted. "As a facilitator, I would not be an *actual* team member, but I'll be closely connected with the team, and especially helping you, the team leader. Again, the facilitator is an expert in team dynamics, and therefore acts as an advisor and teacher, not a team member. The facilitator never *owns* the problem or project, but does have a strong interest in the success of the team. The facilitator doesn't vote or decide on any content-type decisions.

"I've also learned to be extremely careful of not undermining the team leader. It would be very easy for the team members to get confused as to who is really leading the team. The best way to avoid this problem is if I work with you in between meetings to get ready for the *next* meeting. That way, during the meeting itself, you won't need much from me in terms of active intervention in the team dynamics. I would much rather help you behind the scenes.

"Linda, what we just discussed are the basics for leading a special-purpose team. Do you have any questions on any of it?"

"No. I appreciated being able to ask questions along the way to clarify things. I understand what my role will be, but I'm a bit uncertain if I can do it all."

"Don't worry," Dalton responded. "With your personality, intelligence, and hard work, you'll do great. I've every confidence in you. You're sensitive to people, which is a critical skill for leading a team. You're honest and a 'straight-shooter' with others—you do not lie or play games with them. They will *trust* you, which, again, is an absolute essential to being an effective team leader. Finally, I noticed you are very organized, prepared, and task-oriented—very important skills to ensuring a successful team."

Linda, embarrassed by Dalton's unabashed praise, shyly said, "Thank you. I appreciate your help and encouragement. Of course, I also appreciate Matt's confidence in me and his support."

Dalton responded, "I'm very glad to help you with this team. I think we'll all have fun and get plenty accomplished. When I get back to my office, I'll send you some documents from my training summarizing team roles to remind you of our discussion today. You can also share these with the entire team later on to make sure everybody is on the same page."

"Great, thanks!" She then turned to Matt and asked: "Is there anything else I need to do to prepare to launch the team?"

"As I mentioned earlier, Dalton and I discussed having one more meeting with you to review team dynamics. Being aware of how teams function and evolve will help you. Lila will coordinate a time for the three of us before the full team meets."

With that final comment, Linda stood up, shook Dalton's hand, respectfully nodded to Matt, and left the office.

Dalton turned to Matt and said, "I think that went great! I'm more impressed with Linda every time I work with her."

Matt replied, "I agree! She'll do very well with this team, and I think she'll eventually be a great leader for us."

Matt looked at his watch and said, "It's almost lunchtime. Do you want to grab bite to eat? I heard of an interesting restaurant that opened up recently a few blocks away."

Dalton immediately and suspiciously replied, "What do you mean by *interesting*? You're like that Bizarre Foods guy on TV. He eats eyeballs *all the time*. I also still remember the restaurant you took me to that served us a stuffed sheep's stomach!"

Matt, in a fake-hurt and joking tone, retorted, "I'm *nothing* like the Bizarre Foods guy, Andrew Zimmern. I've only had eyeballs *once* in my life, not *all* the time as Zimmern has. Actually, grilled in garlic butter, they are delicious. They have a very satisfying *crunch*. For some reason, they are hard to find in restaurants. . . ." Matt enjoyed seeing Dalton wince as he said "crunch" and continued in a matter-of-fact tone, "In any case, this place I'm thinking about serves Austrian food. They have a delicious Wiener schnitzel, and they don't even serve eyeballs or sheep's stomach."

"Okay," Dalton replied cautiously, "however, I don't plan to eat anything *you* suggest."

They both chuckled at this running joke between them as they walked out the door past a bewildered Lila.

People-Skills Highlighted in This Chapter

Definition of Coaching

In general, a coach instructs a person to achieve a specific goal or skill. In a business environment, coaches help employees improve a specific *business* skill. For example, they may be a sales techniques coach; a coach on specific audit skills, such as report writing; or a coach on teaming skills. No matter what the area of focus, a coach concentrates on improving a few areas at a time. A coaching session is usually an interaction that is planned in advance. In a business setting, supervisors or managers often act as a coach for their employees by teaching them specific skills of the job. However, this role may be assigned to other experts, internal instructors, outside trainers, or more experienced employees. It is very desirable for an organization to have a formal training and development plan that includes coaching on critical skills for job success. New employees should be enrolled in a well-designed onboarding/coaching plan that is tailored to develop the skills they need as quickly as possible.

A coaching session is used as a tool for building up employees, never for tearing them down. It is not an appropriate setting to deliver severe reprimands or sanctions. This is not to say a coach cannot discuss performance gaps in the skills being taught. However, these performance issues should be presented in a way that focuses on skills *development* rather than for punitive purposes.

(continued)

Special-Purpose Team-Leader Role

The management style of the team leader sets the tone for how the team operates. This style should be participative or *delegating* rather than directive, since special-purpose teams are usually composed of highly skilled and self-motivated professionals. The teams are often cross-functional in nature and unlikely to have an official reporting line to the leader, who may be a peer or from a different functional area. Since there are no formal reporting lines, the team leader must work by persuasion and influence rather than by ordering the rest of the team members to take actions.

The team leader must encourage and support the rest of the team to ensure a strong focus on meeting their mission. The leader achieves this by working within the team rather than directing it from above as a manager. To be effective, the leader needs to be respected and trusted by the team members, who must be willing to work together with him or her.

The leader should also have a good understanding of the team's structured process (e.g., problem solving, quality improvement, product development, variability reduction, etc.) being used, and should work very closely with the facilitator, who is the expert on the structured team process.

The leader of a team is a permanent role for the life of the team. The leader is responsible to coordinate and focus the meeting activities on the mission of the team.

The team leader organizes and coordinates the work of the team. As a full-fledged team member, the team leader participates in discussions but is cautious not to dominate them. Often, team leaders are supervisors or managers, although another team member may assume the leader role. The team leader may not be the highest organizationally ranked person on the team. Regardless of their role on a team, managers and supervisors must leave their rank outside the meeting room.

In summary, the leader of a special-purpose team should:

- Focus the team's attention on the objective or goals of the project.
- Serve as the main point of contact with the team sponsor or champion regarding charter negotiations, team progress, reporting, and so on.
- Serve as the team's representative to other internal organizations.
- Work closely with the facilitator to see that team objectives are fulfilled and to develop a plan for upcoming team meetings.
- Serve as a full-fledged team member, acting as a "leader among equals."

- Participate as a member by contributing ideas and taking part in the team processes and decisions.
- Work with the sponsor/champion to remove obstacles, overcome resistance, and obtain resources.
- Schedule the team meetings and ensure all logistics are handled.
- Establish healthy team interaction and encourage participation by team members.
- Ensure that decisions made by the team are carried out.

Situational Leadership Model*

While there are many different leadership models, one valuable leadership style research comes from Paul Hersey and Kenneth Blanchard, which they used to develop their Situational Leadership model. The *Hersey-Blanchard model* concludes that the key to effective leadership is to focus on the attributes and styles of the *followers*.

This model recognizes that different followers have different levels of "competence" and "commitment." The model defines *competence* as ability, knowledge, and skill. *Commitment* is defined as confidence and motivation. These two dimensions are used to describe different levels of development in followers.

In essence, different followers are motivated by different things and have different skill levels, and this must be considered by the leader.

According to Hersey and Blanchard, a good leader develops "the competence and commitment of their people so they're self-motivated rather than dependent on others for direction and guidance." According to the model, four combinations of competence and commitment make up what they called the *development level*:

1. Low competence and low commitment
2. Low competence and high commitment
3. High competence and low/variable commitment
4. High competence and high commitment

The expectation for complex business functions, such as internal audit, is that the practitioners (followers) need to be highly professional. This means they are both very competent and very committed or motivated to accomplish their objectives and tasks. The goal of a good leader in this type of business function is to *develop* followers to the *high competence and high commitment* level.

---

*P. Hersey, and K. H. Blanchard, *Management of Organizational Behavior: Utilizing Human Resources* (Upper Saddle River, NJ: Prentice Hall, 1969).

(continued)

If there is a mismatch between the management style of the leader and the development stage of the follower, there is a great deal of conflict. For example, if the employee is highly capable and motivated, but the manager acts as if the employee needs constant detailed orders, the follower will become very dissatisfied and feel micromanaged. This is likely to demoralize the employee, degrading performance, and perhaps even cause the employee to leave the organization.

The best leadership style for a capable and self-motivated professional in a complex business function is *delegation*. The leader needs to clearly explain and delegate the accomplishment of the goals, and then trust the professional to be motivated and capable enough to accomplish the mission with minimal supervision. The leader will trust that acceptable or even excellent results will be achieved by the employee.

If an employee is not *capable* enough to accomplish the job objectives, then coaching, training, or development activities should be initiated by the leader. If an employee is not sufficiently motivated, then the leader needs to explore possible alternate motivations for the follower. The leaders might be able to provide additional motivation to the employee in the form of opportunities to learn, career growth, raises, bonuses, sense of accomplishment, compliments, public accolades, and so on. In certain circumstances the follower is not only incapable and/or unmotivated, but is unwilling to improve. In this situation, efforts should be made to determine if there is a better fit within the organization, or in the extreme case, terminate employment.

Role of the Team Members

Team members have joint responsibility for achieving the team mission. Members typically have expertise in the required technical skills to accomplish the mission. Team members are usually selected because they represent a part of the cross-functional process that is being improved or developed. Sometimes, a team member from outside of the process is included to give a fresh perspective. Members should participate in discussions, provide suggestions, make joint decisions, and do other tasks such as gathering data, analyzing information, creating processes, and assisting with documentation. Ideally, teams usually have four to eight members, including the team leader. The team may be larger, but larger teams usually take longer to reach consensus and accomplish their mission.

In summary, team members should:

■ Work diligently to achieve the team mission.
■ Treat team participation as an important part of their job.

- Respect and constructively work with other team members, team leader, facilitator, and team sponsor.
- Attend all team meetings and understand the team mission has a high priority.
- Develop and adhere to the team ground rules.
- Provide process/technical knowledge and expertise.
- Contribute as actively as possible.
- Carry out team assignments as committed.
- Help analyze process data.
- Provide ideas and creative input to solutions.

Team Sponsor or Champion Role

The team sponsor, or team *champion*, is the member of management who usually identifies the need for the team, launches the team, and supports the team to achieve the mission.

In summary, the team champion or sponsor should:

- Formally commission the team.
- Select the team members, appoint a *team leader*, and arrange for a *team facilitator*.
- Clarify the mission, identify project boundaries, and set broad team objectives.
- Encourage the team to meet objectives on time.
- Coordinate with required managers and other executives for availability of personnel.
- Serve as the team's main point of contact with the leaders of other organizations and/or upper management for charter or resource negotiations.
- Provide the team with required resources.
- Work closely with the team leader to monitor team progress.
- With team input, make the strategic decisions around the team direction and timing of milestones, including final accomplishment of the mission.
- Formally approve the accomplishment of team milestones and key documents (e.g., mission statement) before the team progresses to the next milestones.
- Help overcome resistance from employees or managers outside the team.
- Gain approval by upper management to implement team recommendations.

(continued)

Team Facilitator Role

Facilitators are skilled communicators who are knowledgeable about team dynamics and interaction. They assist the team in achieving its objectives by guiding the team. The facilitator should be an objective team resource who is detached from the process being improved. This allows the facilitator to remain active in process and neutral on content. The facilitator is not an actual team member, but is closely connected with the team, and especially with the team leader. This person is an expert in teaming and in the structured improvement process, and thus acts as an advisor, coach, and teacher. The facilitator never owns the problem, but always has a strong interest in the success of the team.

An effective facilitator may lead the team in specific activities, yet does not undermine the leader's role. The facilitator is introduced by the team leader or sponsor as someone who will help the team achieve the objectives by leading them through a specific structured activity. The facilitator should be an expert in the tools and methodology needed by the team. For example, if the team mission is to reduce waste in a process or reduce variability, then the facilitator should be an expert, perhaps a Blackbelt, at Six Sigma and Lean techniques.

The most effective teams have a trained team facilitator in a permanent role to meet with them and guide their use of meeting skills and tools. The facilitator should be present at most meetings, but especially in the early stages of development when the team is learning how to work together. The involvement of the facilitator normally diminishes as the team members and team leader gain more knowledge and skills about team processes and tools.

The facilitator must exercise discipline to avoid inappropriate participation in the team decisions.

In summary, the team facilitator should:

- Maintain a climate conducive to listening, learning, participating, and creating.
- Assist the team in reaching decisions, coming to a consensus, defining next steps, and achieving timely completion of the mission.
- Work with the team leader to plan meetings, and structure assignments.
- Challenge members to be open with each other and resolve differences in a constructive manner.
- Keep the team on track by helping them follow the ground rules they established.
- Encourage the group to evaluate its own effectiveness by leading periodic team self-assessment activities.

6

Team Dynamics: Setting the Foundation for Success

People-Centric Skills

Team Dynamics; Stages of Team Development; Team Ground Rules; Team Mission Statement; Building Consensus

D ALTON AND LINDA arrived at 7:00 A.M. at Matt's office, escorted by Lila. All four simultaneously mumbled a sleepy "Good morning."

Matt waved Dalton and Linda in and indicated his small table on the side of his office and said, "Thanks, Lila! I think we will need lots of coffee today. Dalton and Linda, thanks for coming in so early to plan the launch of the R&M audit development team. I have back-to-back meetings today, so, this is all of my availability for the day."

After shaking hands with Matt, Dalton sat down, adjusted his vest, rummaged through his bag, and handed Linda and Matt a document. "Since our time is limited, let's jump right in. Linda, as we discussed last time, today we'll focus on the skills you will need to launch your team next week. You did attend my P-C Skills class where we covered teaming at a high level; today, I plan to expound upon it. This document is what I included in my class and should help you recollect some of the key points. You probably remember that I really like Tuckman's Four-Phase model on team development. He did a lot of research into understanding what teams go through and what makes teams successful. Tuckman developed the theory that there are four distinct stages of team development, and every successful team goes through them.

"The first stage is called the *Forming* stage. At this point, the group is getting a feel for each other. Each team member's behavior is driven by a desire to be accepted by the others and avoid conflict. Team members are also forming impressions about each other and about the scope of the task and how to approach it. Not much will get accomplished at this stage. Frankly, one of the things I worry about in this team is what seems to be a somewhat strained working relationship between you and Meghan. That strain might get in the way of properly *forming* the team. I suggest you have a conversation with her and try to clear the air so you can establish a good rapport. You all must work together for the team to succeed. Meghan's a professional, so I believe she will work with you just fine; but when emotions get involved in any situation, it's hard to tell how somebody will react."

Linda nodded slowly at this and carefully chose her words. "I know that Meghan and I have struggled a bit with each other. We have such different personalities. However, we are both professional and I'm sure we'll work it out. She actually approached me awhile back and offered to be a mentor to me, and I gladly accepted, so I think we are already on our way. I'll see if she can join me for lunch today so we can discuss how to improve our relationship further, especially in light of this project. Food always helps with any interaction!"

Both Dalton and Matt were impressed with Linda's nondefensive and positive approach to addressing this situation. Matt particularly liked her "food always helps" sentiment. They had agreed ahead of time that both Linda and Meghan needed to be approached separately to encourage better relations.

Dalton continued, "I think lunch with Meghan is a great idea. Before I forget my train of thought, let me continue with the stages of teaming. So, the first stage again is Forming and then the second stage is the *Storming* stage. This is characterized by conflict and interpersonal problems. Team members open up to each other, but their views might be harshly challenged by the rest of the team. In some cases, Storming can be resolved quickly. In other instances, the team never leaves this stage. The maturity and interpersonal skills of the team members and the leader usually determine whether the team ever moves out of this stage. Some team members will focus on minutiae to evade real issues. It can be argumentative, unpleasant, and even painful to team members who are averse to conflict. Tolerance of each team member and their differences needs to be emphasized. As the team leader, you should be very aware of any conflict between team members and then work behind the scenes to resolve the conflicts. You can call on me or Matt if you want to discuss approaches to this.

"The third stage is the *Norming* stage. At this point, resistance is overcome and group feelings of cohesiveness develop, new team rules evolve as the team decides how they want to work together, and member roles are firmed up. Now, personal opinions are comfortably expressed and, to a certain extent, conflict is avoided. Team members handle differences in a more constructive and non-defensive manner. Teams must watch out for Groupthink here. As you might remember from my P-C training, Groupthink is when team members agree to something they don't believe in just so that they get along with the others. While this maintains the peace, it's much better if people can openly express different opinions and then work together on a common approach. Otherwise, the team may be missing valuable ideas that aren't stated.

"Finally, if the members have done the right things, the team attains the fourth and final stage, the *Performing* stage. This is the phase where the real accomplishments are made by successful teams. Roles become flexible and functional, and group energy is channeled into accomplishing the mission rather than battling each other. Team members can easily express their opinions; conflict is managed quickly and constructively; decisions are made in a natural and smooth manner; and everybody realizes that to succeed as individuals, they will need to succeed jointly in their team task. Reaching this stage as quickly as possible should be the goal for every team."

At this point, Dalton paused and took a deep breath to give Linda a chance to comment, which she immediately did: "I remember going over this in your class, and it all makes sense with the experiences I've had in the past. However, since all teams go through these four stages, what is the point of facilitation? Won't teams evolve on their own to the final stage? I think I know the answer, but I'd rather be really sure about this."

Dalton smiled widely and responded, "That's *exactly* the right question. The *successful* teams go all the way through the four stages to the Performing stage. Some unsuccessful teams get to the Storming stage and can't break out of it. These teams have so much conflict, distrust, and lack of common purpose that they fail. Some teams muddle through to the Norming stage, but don't progress to the Performing stage. These teams might generate an output, but not necessarily a great output. Finally, even if teams push all the way to the Performing stage, it might take them forever to get there. They could generate a great result, but in a very slow and inefficient manner. To succeed, businesses need to get to the best answer as quickly and as efficiently as possible. *That's* where facilitation and good understanding of team dynamics come in. With my assistance, and your team leadership, we will get through the four stages as quickly and as smoothly as possible, so your team can *perform* its mission."

Both Linda and Matt nodded emphatically all the way through Dalton's last statement. Linda then added, "Thanks for that explanation. It confirms for me that I understood. Succeeding in this team is very important to me and to Internal Audit. So, how do we get started?"

Dalton then launched into a flurry of advice. "The auditors on your team went through my P-C course, so, they should be familiar with the team dynamics concepts and the stages of teaming. However, the engineers on the team haven't. I propose that Matt introduces me and my role to the team, provides the initial high-level project goals, and clearly endorses you as the team leader. I'll then go into trainer mode for a couple of hours. I'll clearly explain the four stages of teaming, the importance of moving through them as quickly as possible, and then make suggestions for initial team activities to set the conditions for success.

"I think you should first ask everybody to introduce themselves in a very comprehensive manner. The jobs they had, what they studied, what they are responsible for right now, the skills they have developed, their preferred work styles, their interests, hobbies, family . . . the full works. However, you should tell them to avoid politics and religion. These topics are not appropriate in a work setting and can be very divisive. Besides these two topics, the more people know about each other, the more they tend to trust each other. You should start so they understand what depth you expect them to go to. This will help everybody see each other's roles and understand how they can contribute to the team. The faster the team members get to know each other well, the more trust you'll have in other team members, and the faster you'll go through the team stages. This type of full introduction will turbo-charge the getting-to-know-each-other phase. Have fun with it! Give some little known facts and lighten the mood a bit from the onset. For the same reason, you should invite everybody out to dinner and meals as much as possible. In an informal dinner setting, you can get to know your team members as people, and not just business colleagues."

At this suggestion Linda raised one eyebrow and quizzically looked at Matt as she realized there might be budget issues with dinners. She knew Matt was always prudent with MultiCrown money. Matt looked back at her, envious he couldn't raise one eyebrow himself. Such a useful mannerism! When he was a young professional, he remembered trying to do this in front of a mirror with no success. He always looked like he had a toothache—not the image he wanted to project. With some effort, Matt snapped out of his reverie. "Dinner together makes sense. The engineers are our guests *and* doing us a favor. Please select the places carefully—casual restaurants might be more conducive to getting to know each other, and hopefully, are less painful on our budget. Also, please watch the alcohol intake. You know how wild engineers and auditors can get when they party together!" All three smirked at this, and Dalton picked up the conversation again.

"After the introductions and my team dynamics overview, I suggest you all work together to create the Team Ground Rules. Assign a team member to write these rules down as the team develops them and make sure the rules can be seen by everyone. A laptop and projector work well, but if not, regular flipcharts are fine. I can facilitate this if you want, but you probably won't need my help. Basically, you want to get everybody to agree on how the team members will want to operate and how they should behave. A quick rule of thumb: If everyone on the team begins to take personal notes, it shows a lack of trust. On the other hand, if it's delegated to one designated team member, this might be an indicator that this team will come together quickly. This will move you faster through the Storming stage since having a clear understanding of the rules will reduce needless conflict.

"The Team Ground Rules can cover a broad range of topics such as how the decisions will be made—will it be by full consensus, or by majority vote, or by Matt's edict?; the expectations for punctuality to team meetings; how the team will communicate with each other; the frequency and length of team meetings; in person or remotely via videoconferencing? How will minutes be taken? What about agreeing to the milestone dates for accomplishing the various portions of the R&M audit program? What are the expectations for completing assignments on time? How will assignment results be communicated? By the way, I suggest you set up a SharingBox on the MultiCrown cloud where team documents can be updated, viewed, and edited by all team members. Matt can also monitor progress by looking over the team documents. The Ground Rules should be a living document. The team can add to it and change the rules as needed and as agreed to by the team."

Dalton was impressed by Linda's buy-in and sharp focus on the conversation. He had been through many similar conversations in the past, and some of the project leaders thought they knew how to run a team—believing all of this proverbial red tape wasn't necessary. Dalton had learned on numerous occasions that without this red tape, team dynamics are difficult to work through. Without *formalizing* rules, they will be broken. It is the same with policies—people know what to do, but without guidance, human nature often prevails and we tend to do whatever we want.

"After you set up the Team Ground Rules, I suggest that Matt gives a detailed description of his prior experience in developing an R&M audit function and what he hopes to get out of your team. People can then ask Matt all the clarification questions they want. After this is done, Matt should probably leave, and the team can formally write a concise mission statement so that everybody on the team is clearly on the same page. Matt would then return and formally approve your mission statement. In essence, how will you recognize success after you achieve it? What will be your key performance indicators or KPIs? This will again speed you through the teaming stages. I've seen teams struggle for months because they didn't all have the same understanding of their mission. I can help facilitate this, but Linda should be taking the clear lead on this effort."

Linda thought about what Dalton has recommended on the Ground Rules. "Dalton, this all makes sense. Let me think about the types of items we may want in the Ground Rules so I can lead the discussion. I won't pre-decide anything, since this is the prerogative of the full team, but I can make sure we cover all the needed topics. After I draft this, can I send it to you for your thoughts?"

"Sure thing. I'll also send you a write-up on Team Ground Rules I have in my files. Can we break for a refill on coffee? I'm parched."

After glancing at his watch, Matt said. "Why don't the two of you go ahead on the coffee and feel free to continue to discuss the team launch here in my office? I need to run to another meeting."

· · ·

A week had passed since the last prep meeting with Linda. Matt was in the Audit conference room with the three Internal Audit team members: Meghan, Sandra, and Linda. Sandra had arrived last night from Brazil, but she seemed perky enough after her long trip. With them were the three maintenance engineers representing three of MultiCrown's divisions. They were acting a bit lost as they huddled together at one end of the table, seemingly for mutual support. Matt speculated they were wondering what they'd done to deserve being locked up in a room full of auditors for the next three days, although he had carefully explained the project as part of his earlier communications.

They were all munching on bagels and cream cheese thoughtfully provided by Lila. With every bite of her bagel and cream cheese, Sandra softly muttered an unconscious "*Mmmm . . .*" in apparent pleasure. Maybe it was tough to find good bagels in Sao Paulo. Matt hoped Sandra would finish her bagel before Dalton arrived. Sandra's constant *mmmm*'s would likely distract Dalton, who was easily distracted where Sandra was concerned. Matt looked at the clock and saw that Dalton was 20 minutes late, but this had been a good time for the audit managers to start to get to know the engineers.

Finally, Dalton rushed in, escorted by Lila. He immediately filled the room with his exuberant presence. Dalton apologized right away, "I'm *really* sorry I'm late. A truck full of caged chickens turned over in the middle of the Kennedy Expressway! Some escaped and were running around all over the place! Drivers were swerving to avoid the chickens—feathers *everywhere*—what a mess!"

At this outburst from Dalton, Lila giggled, Meghan smirked, Linda laughed, Sandra chuckled, and Matt smiled. The three engineers seemed confused and baffled by the whirlwind who was Dalton.

Sandra asked in a disbelieving tone, "On some small dirt roads in Brazil there are trucks with chickens, but in downtown Chicago?"

Matt realized he'd better get control of the meeting, otherwise, they would be discussing chickens all morning. Matt also remembered that Dalton told him something months ago that might explain why he was always running a little late. Dalton's theory was that he likes to put people in somewhat uncomfortable situations to see how they handle them. Maybe this was why Dalton was late sometimes. Or most likely, Dalton needed an executive assistant. At this, his mind drifted to the dreadful possibility that Dalton might try to steal Lila away.

With a disciplined refocus on the meeting, Matt quickly started the introductions. "Dalton, glad you made it, given your unforeseen chicken challenges. Of course, you remember the auditors? Let me also introduce you to our guests, who are probably wondering what the heck they got themselves into. Representing the Plastics Molding division is Trey Poltec," Matt made a discreet hand signal toward a tall, thin gentleman with a mustache. "From the Advanced Ceramics division, this is Kirk Carter," gesturing to a fireplug-looking powerful man, short in stature and the same width from top to bottom. Turning to the last engineer, "And this is Chester Turnbull, representing the Metals Matrix and Composite division." He gestured to a tall, fit African-American gentleman with a shaved head and a big smile.

Dalton in turn shook hands with all three. While rubbing his own shaved head, he complimented Chester on his wonderful hair and then sat at ease next to Matt, but strategically facing Sandra. Dalton found it very interesting that Trey and Chester had very "normal," firm handshakes—solid and not too sweaty, and not dominating at all. Kirk, however, began to turn his hand to the top once he began to shake Dalton's hand. Knowing this to be a strategy of some people to show power, Dalton wondered what power Kirk was trying to show. Maybe he had a bit of a Napoleon complex.

Making eye contact with each of them, Matt began. "Thank you all for being here; I know this is a big commitment of time for all of you." Addressing the three engineers, he continued, "When I invited you to this meeting, I explained what our goal was, and that your division president volunteered each of you as one of the best maintenance leaders of your division. As I mentioned, I selected Linda to be the team leader for this effort."

At this comment, Meghan made a slight frown, and it reminded Matt he still needed to meet with Meghan and explain the assignment was made to help develop Linda. He knew he needed to reassure Meghan this was not an implied criticism of her own leadership. Maybe it would make Meghan feel more engaged if he would remind her that part of mentoring was actively helping to develop Linda's leadership skills.

Dalton also noticed the frown; but, in addition, took in the other signs that betrayed her mood: the rigid posture, minimal eye contact, and pursed lips. These were telltale signs of defensiveness. Dalton met Matt's eyes and knew they both saw the need to tackle this potential problem.

After this fleeting thought about Meghan, Matt continued, "Dalton will act as the team facilitator. He's an expert consultant on teaming and communications, and we'll cover his role in much greater depth later on. I'm the team sponsor, and, given I've done this type of R&M audit project in my past, I'll also act as a technical advisor from time to time. As part of the session today, Linda will discuss the main team roles so we know what to expect from each other." Matt paused to see if there were any questions, and then gestured to Linda. "Linda, why don't you take it from here?"

She started with apparent confidence and enthusiasm. "Thank you all for being here. I'm really looking forward to working with all of you on this team and accomplishing our mission. I thought we'd start out with really in-depth introductions. As Dalton has advised me, the faster and deeper we get to know each other, the better the team members can establish trust and make progress. We want to know not only about your experience, skills, jobs, and training, but also hobbies, interests, family, amusing anecdotes, and so on. I can start out and then Dalton and Matt will introduce themselves. By the way, Dalton suggested we stay away from politics or religion in our introductions. I'm sure you can see why."

The team members spent the next hour and a half with the in-depth introductions. As the introductions continued, the team members began to relax as they realized they were no longer sitting with strangers. They chuckled in appreciation at some of the interesting hobbies and activities they heard about each other.

Linda was a self-described "techno-nerd" and was always the first in line to buy the latest electronic gadgets. She liked to read science fiction and attended many sci-fi conventions. She sheepishly admitted that sometimes, she even went in a Princess Leia costume. She was also active in "Save the Children" and several environmental organizations.

Meghan had a black-belt in Judo, enjoyed mountain climbing, and was a local newspaper and magazine model while in college. She was also captain of her college debate team.

Sandra had been on Brazil's Olympic fencing team, and her parents are from a long line of circus knife throwers. She was an expert on the saber and the epée. She also danced in Sao Paulo's Carnival parade every year as part of a samba group.

Dalton was full of eclectic but quirky interests. His most unusual experience dealt with how he had once either been chased by a brown bear or had chased a bear—he was a bit vague about this. Dalton could go on for hours, being an extrovert. Additionally, his vast travel experience was fodder for great stories. Matt noticed how Sandra's ears perked up when Dalton mentioned his yoga and meditation interests.

Matt had a lifelong interest in cooking international foods and seemed to be obsessed with exotic spices, herbs, and ingredients. Some of the team members shuddered at the unusual items Matt had tried, like the grilled goathead in Northern Mexico, or the salty fried grasshoppers he had had in Central America. Even Dalton looked a bit green when Matt described eating these "delicacies." He was an avid reader, and enjoyed science magazines, business journals and blogs, murder mysteries, and science fiction. Matt also mentioned his 20 years of Aikido, although he no longer competed in tournaments.

Chester played trombone in a jazz ensemble and liked to skydive. He had eight brothers and sisters, and had four children of his own. As he described the personalities of his kids, it was obvious how family oriented he was.

Trey ran marathons. He had been a basketball star while in college and was still an active basketball player in a neighborhood league. He was also an avid chess player.

Powerful and stocky Kirk Carter liked to do origami and Japanese calligraphy in his spare time, in addition to coaching all of his kids' sports.

With a satisfied sigh, Linda smiled broadly at the team. "Thank you for your great introductions. I'm now even more excited to be working with all of you. What an interesting group! How about a 15-minute break and then Dalton can give us an overview of the stages of team development and other teaming topics. We'll meet back here at 10:30."

For about two hours after the break, Dalton presented the four stages of teaming. The auditors had heard most of this before in Dalton's training, but it was all new to the engineers. Although the auditors could have been bored by the repetition, they were paying close attention now that they had to put these theories into practice. Dalton also had the innate ability to make things interesting, regardless of whether the material was duplicative. The engineers were fascinated to learn that teams *have* structure and consistent stages of development. Being engineers, they appreciated orderly structure and consistency. Finally, after covering the team stages, and fielding numerous questions and comments, Dalton paused and raised his eyebrows to see what else the team members had to say.

After an uncertain moment, Meghan jumped in, addressing the full team. "So, bottom line: The faster we get to the Performing stage the more productive and successful we'll be. There are no real shortcuts, we can't skip a stage, but if we are good enough, and we do the preparation and activities Dalton suggests, we can move past the earlier stages much faster."

Dalton beamed, "Perfect! Great summary—I might steal it for my next P-C class. I particularly liked your comment on 'doing what Dalton suggests'!"

Chester, with some shyness, remarked in his deep baritone, "I guess that's why we went through such a deep introduction. So we'd move faster through the Forming stage and we could then handle the Storming stage in a better fashion." Dalton again beamed at his attentive students. "That's it! Not only to get through the first two stages, but to go through *all* stages more effectively. Again, *trust* between the team members is the magic stuff. The better you know each other *and* understand you're all pushing for the success of the team, the more you'll be able to trust the others to do their part."

Dalton spent the next hour covering, in detail, the roles of the team sponsor, team leader, facilitator, and team members. While there were a few questions, for the most part they listened attentively. When Dalton wound down, it was evident that the roles were clearly understood and accepted by all.

Dalton wrapped up this section, stating, "These team roles are pretty logical after you hear about them, but I have seen teams falter because of a lack of understanding of these roles, particularly if there is confusion as to what the team leader is supposed to do or not do."

Linda glanced at the team members and decided it was time to gently reassert her leadership role. She quietly said, "Now that we have the theory in place, let's get to a very important initial effort for our team. This is developing the Team Ground Rules. Basically, it's our agreement and commitment as to how we'll work together. Good Ground Rules reduce uncertainty and help prevent conflicts. This means we get past the storming stage as quickly and painlessly as possible. Is anybody willing to connect their laptop to the projector and take notes on our proposed Ground Rules?"

As she looked around, she was happy to see several half-raised hands. She smiled at Meghan, and quietly uttered, "Thanks, Meghan, it's great that you'll take the notes today." Linda was pleased that the lunch she and Meghan had had together seemed to have been good for their relationship, and saw Meghan volunteering to take notes as a very good sign. However, Linda did realize that she and Meghan would need to do much more to establish a solid relationship. Dalton caught Matt's eyes and they both nodded imperceptibly to each other at Meghan's offer.

Just as Dalton had advised at their prep meeting, Linda stood next to the projector screen with a four-foot pointer to reinforce her team leadership. "So, the first thing we need to decide is when to meet and how often to meet. Given we are scattered all over the world, we should use videoconferencing for most meetings. Any thoughts?" The next 15 minutes were filled with everybody checking their calendars on their smart phones and throwing out suggestions and objections. Finally, they all agreed to meet once a week, on Tuesday mornings from 9:00 A.M. to 11:00 A.M. Central Time, with Linda setting up and initiating the videoconference calls.

Linda, pleased that their first decision, although a small one, went smoothly, continued, "Now that we have a meeting time, can we commit via our Ground Rules that our team meetings will take priority over other time demands? I know that sometimes we can't control our schedule, but if we start missing team meetings, we won't be able to progress as we need to."

Meghan and Sandra nodded in agreement, but Trey commented, "The auditors here work for Matt, who supports this project as a high-priority effort. But, we engineers have bosses who might not see it that way. Matt, could you send a note to our bosses stating that the division presidents have agreed to this project and asking them to support us carving out this time on Tuesdays? I think it will help us to not get pulled into other meetings by our bosses." The two other engineers, Kirk and Chester, immediately agreed. Matt replied, "Sure, Trey. I was going to send a note to your bosses, anyway, to thank them for allowing you to participate in this project, and I'll definitely mention the Tuesday meetings and specifically thank them for keeping this time clear for you."

With the satisfied nods from the three engineers, Meghan added a bullet to the Ground Rules list right below the Tuesday-morning meeting time: "The team meetings will take priority over other time demands."

Linda commented, "Good. Now let's move on to how we make team decisions. Consensus? Majority voting? Matt decides?"

As they all thought about this, Dalton suggested, "Listen, I've worked with a great many teams, and maybe I can save you some time. Let me propose something and you can then accept it, reject it, or use it as a starting point. Matt is too busy to make all team decisions. Since he won't be at most meetings, he won't even have the background to make the decisions. I suggest Matt make the decisions for critical strategies and objectives—using your team's recommendations, of course. For important, but not strategic, team decisions, I suggest you reach full consensus as a team—the same as a jury might. This may take longer, but then everybody will be able to buy into the decision. Remember that consensus does not mean that it's the decision *preferred* by *each* of you, only that all of you are willing to live with the decision and support it. If you really get stuck and can't reach consensus, then you can ask Matt for his thoughts, but you should work hard to minimize this. Finally, for simple procedural decisions, it's okay to have a quick show of hands as a vote. Unless somebody really disagrees, then just go with the majority vote."

Dalton then paused to see their reaction. He was glad when Sandra spoke up. Actually, he was always glad when Sandra did anything. Smiling to tease him a bit, she suggested, "Given Dalton's vast experience with teams—over many decades, probably—I think we should follow his advice."

With everyone nodding at this, Meghan added another bullet to the Ground Rules: "*Team Decisions*: Strategic decisions, by Matt. Important decisions, by team consensus. Procedural decisions, by simple majority vote (unless somebody objects)."

Linda then commented, "That's a great summary, Meghan. Our decision on how to make decisions needs to be agreed to by full consensus. Any thoughts or objections?" With nods all around, Linda continued, "We all agree? Great!"

Over the next hour or so, the team agreed to a number of other Team Ground Rules, which Meghan faithfully added to their growing list. There were some spirited differences of opinions along the way, but they quickly ironed the differences out, and all generally seemed pleased with the list:

R&M/Audit Team—Ground Rules
- Team meetings on Tuesday mornings from 9:00 A.M. to 11:00 A.M. Central Time via videoconference calls.

- Linda to arrange and initiate the videoconference calls.
- Team meetings will take priority over other time demands.
- *Team Decisions:* Strategic decisions, by Matt. Important decisions, by team consensus. Procedural decisions, by simple vote unless somebody objects (if so, then discuss and work toward consensus).
- All team members (and Dalton!) agreed to be punctual and not be more than five minutes late to any meeting. (Chickens on the road are not a valid excuse!)
- A minutes-taker will be identified for each team meeting. This role will rotate among team members, except for Linda.
- Everybody will try to avoid, as much as possible, taking phone calls or checking emails during meetings.
- Team documents will be stored in a team SharingBox on the MultiCrown cloud. Linda will be responsible for setting and maintaining the folder structure for the documents.
- Team documents can be updated, viewed, and edited by everybody on the team.
- Completed assignments will be uploaded to the SharingBox at least 24 hours before the Tuesday meetings so other team members can read and digest before any discussion.
- Matt will monitor team progress by reviewing the team documents and minutes, in discussions with Linda.
- Specific project milestone dates will be established, and Matt will formally approve the accomplishment of each milestone before the team progresses further.
- If the team wants help, Dalton will be asked if he could facilitate at a specific Tuesday meeting.
- Conversations or opinions stated during team meetings will not be shared with anybody outside the team. Likewise, minutes or team documents will not be shared with others unless approved by the team.
- We will always treat each other with respect. We will trust each other. We will listen to different opinions in a nondefensive manner. We will assume that all team members want the team and MultiCrown to succeed.

Linda glanced at the clock. In a very satisfied and enthusiastic tone, she exclaimed, "We have done a great job with this list. Meghan, thanks again for your help. Lila ordered lunch for us, and we have pizza and salad in the kitchen. Let's take an hour to eat, check emails, or whatever, and continue our meeting at 2:00 P.M." With this, everybody rushed to the kitchen, with Dalton leading the way. Matt politely waved everybody to go ahead of him and trailed the team. With Lila ordering the food, he knew there would still be plenty of anchovy pizza by the time he got to prepare his plate.

After the lunch break, Matt resumed, "I thought it would be useful for me to give you an overview of the R&M audit effort I led in a prior company. I learned some important lessons as we rolled out our R&M audits, and I hope your team takes an open and fresh look at this effort. However, I think it will be helpful for you to hear what was been done in the past before you create your own Team Mission Statement and lay out the Team Milestones. Most of this overview will be very familiar to Trey, Kirk, and Chester, but may be very new to the auditors." Addressing the engineers, Matt said, "Gentlemen, please feel free to add any additional comments as we go along, you are the experts!"

"To start out, an effective Repair and Maintenance function, or R&M, is critically important in many industries. These include manufacturing, transportation, mining, metals, pharmaceuticals, medical devices, airlines, chemicals, and so forth. Basically, any industry that operates equipment needs a capable R&M function, and this certainly includes MultiCrown. We spend over $800 million each year on R&M, so you can see that even minor improvements in our processes could add up to big savings. Also, even small process inefficiencies can cost us a lot of money." At this comment, all three engineers nodded emphatically. They appreciated that Matt started out by highlighting the importance of their profession.

Noting the nods, Matt continued, "A good R&M function reduces capital expenditures because equipment that's well maintained lasts much longer than equipment poorly maintained. If you doubt this, stop changing the oil in your car! Also, with proper R&M, critical equipment is less likely to fail, thereby stopping production. If we can't produce a product, we can't sell it; and then there's no revenue, no profit, and of course, *no bonuses*." He thought the "bonuses" comment should make the opportunities more personal and catch their attention. Noting their intent facial expressions he went on, "Properly maintained equipment also helps meet quality standards and is critical to customer satisfaction. Finally, it's usually much more cost-effective to maintain equipment than to repair it once it's broken.

"So, given the importance of R&M, what can auditors do to help improve this technical function? There is really very little an auditor can tell a maintenance engineer on how to *technically* maintain or restore a piece of equipment. This is beyond most auditors' skills." With this comment, the three engineers again nodded their heads in emphatic agreement, but no one said anything, waiting to see how Matt would explain the auditors' role in R&M.

Matt acknowledged the nods and continued, "However, there is a lot an auditor can do to review and test the R&M *processes* to help improve this area. Auditors are experts at well-managed processes and should recognize what it takes to capably execute a function. With some research, and this team's guidance, auditors should be able to recommend improvements that would enhance the efficiency and effectiveness of our R&M *processes*. This improvement goal is an integral part of the audit profession's definition of Internal Audit." This time, it was the three auditors who nodded, but remained silent.

"I'm sure Trey, Kirk, and Chester will add much more to my summary in future meetings, but I wanted to highlight various key elements that well-run R&M organizations should have. Using these concepts as a basis, your team could design an operational audit program that's tailored to the exact needs of MultiCrown.

"In my past role as the head of Audit for a $20 billion global industrial company with hundreds of manufacturing locations, I invited our three best R&M engineers to join me and two audit managers for a team effort that resulted in our R&M audit program. This effort also generated a guide that became the reference material for auditors. For the first several audits, the R&M experts on the development team joined the audits as 'guest auditors' and were paired with senior auditors. This served as a way to validate the R&M audit program and facilitate knowledge transfer to Audit. The R&M audit effort resulted in many valuable audit recommendations, and was acknowledged by the CEO as an example of how good operational auditing can contribute to the bottom line. I'll gladly tell you more about my experience with this prior R&M audit effort at later meetings."

Before Matt could go on, Chester asked, "Could you share some of those R&M audit recommendations with us? It might help us understand where we're going with this." After a moment, Matt, with some hesitancy about possibly revealing confidential material from another company, replied, "Let me see what I can come up with. I can probably generate a list of 10 or 12 common types of R&M audit recommendations for the team to see."

"Thanks, Matt, I think it will really help us."

"No problem, Chester. It was a very good suggestion. Let me go on with the R&M basics. One important element of an effective R&M function is a system that has information on the equipment of the facility. The system should be able to hold information such as: How critical is the individual equipment to overall production? When did it break down last? How often does the equipment fail? How long did it take to repair, and how costly was it? Are spare parts with a long-lead-time horizon needed, and are they available in stock? What's the history of maintenance for the equipment? Another important module of a good R&M system is that it has a scheduling function with the date of the next maintenance event for each piece of equipment. Every morning, a report should be generated by the system with the day's scheduled maintenance events for the engineers to follow. So my questions for Kirk, Trey, and Chester are: Does MultiCrown have such systems? How are they working? Could they be better?"

The three maintenance engineers looked at each other as if uncertain how to answer. Finally, Kirk spoke up in a gravelly voice. "We do have a system in our division, but it's pretty antiquated and different plants use it to a different degree. I think we use it as effectively as possible at the R&M department I manage. The auditors could really help the entire Advanced Ceramics Division if you could encourage the other units to use the system in a more effective fashion. I tried to suggest that we form a group of our division's R&M managers to drive best practices in system usage, but my suggestion didn't go anywhere."

"It's a coincidence," Trey added, "but last night, Kirk, Chester, and I discussed our R&M systems and the inconsistent ways they are being used. Each division has a different system, but they are all pretty old. If the R&M/Audit team's project can help us in just this one area, the entire effort on our part would be worth it. Actually, what we'd ideally hope is that once Internal Audit looks at the R&M practices at enough plants, you might recommend to our CEO that MultiCrown could really benefit from an investment in a modern system we could all use."

As if on a swivel, the heads of the three engineers simultaneously turned to expectantly look at Matt. He cleared his throat, giving himself a few seconds to think before carefully responding. "Well, if we really find good opportunities in a new system, and if the engineers and accountants could work together to properly justify it financially, I'd gladly suggest it to our CEO. Caleb is always open to improvements. A leading system, consistently used, would not only help each of our facilities, but would allow each division and even the entire company to analyze and improve R&M practices across the board. For example, expensive spare parts could be centralized into geographic regions to reduce cost. However, to make this work, you need a good system. Perhaps after this team's mission is accomplished, we could reconstitute the team with the new mission of analyzing the R&M system options. To maintain auditor independence, this project would need to be *driven* by the R&M people, with the auditors acting as advisors. However, behind the scenes, I could act as a quiet champion for this effort. Again, only if we can prove that the project returns are over MultiCrown's investment threshold."

The engineers seemed to be very satisfied by Matt's support, although they noted there were some careful caveats included. The auditors looked at each other, realizing that even though the team had barely gotten started, they were already identifying possible opportunities for MultiCrown.

Linda spoke up, "How about if we add a possible new R&M system to our Idea Parking Lot to make sure the suggestion doesn't get lost?" She then took a few minutes to describe this tool for the team, with Dalton making a few encouraging comments. After the team agreed, she wrote "New R&M system" on a flipchart.

Matt went on, "This new project could be a great possibility for us down the line, but let me go on with the process attributes of good R&M departments. We only just covered the use of an R&M system. Again, I apologize to the engineers since you are likely to be bored."

"To cover some basics, *repair* is when you fix something *after* it has failed and the equipment isn't operating. *Preventive maintenance* is the strategy used to work on the equipment *before* it fails to *prevent* it from failing. Based on engineering studies, past failures, benchmarking data, and information from the equipment manufacturer, an estimate is made of the interval between failures and when the equipment is likely to fail next. The maintenance activity is then scheduled for a conservative period before failure is anticipated. The more painful the possible failure, the more conservative the advanced interval for maintenance should be. While this type of maintenance is certainly much less costly than having critical failures, it does leave money on the table. You are basically replacing parts and equipment *before* they fail, so you waste any remaining useful life that they have. Maintenance management should perform a cost-benefit analysis considering the probability and cost of equipment failure versus the cost of wasted life of the replaced equipment. The auditors can certainly assess this analysis as part of their work."

Matt again turned to the engineers. "Any thoughts on this?"

This time, Trey answered first. "I wish we always had the thorough scientific and economic analysis you mentioned to determine the useful life of a piece of equipment before we decide it needs to be replaced or maintained. I think some of our shops are flying by the seat of their pants on this, and may be wasting money."

Kirk jumped in. "At our division we do it much better. We have careful analysis and calculations to determine the optimal preventive maintenance schedule."

Trey seemed to bristle at Kirk's immediate assertion of superiority. Dalton, observing this, wondered if this was the beginning of the Storming stage for the team.

Apparently oblivious to the tension between Trey and Kirk, Chester added, "I think some of our plants do a good job of determining the preventive maintenance periods and others don't. However, I've noticed that a number of our plants often miss *performing* the preventive maintenance tasks *as scheduled*. They always seem to be behind their plan. Maybe this is due to shortage of maintenance engineers."

At this, Matt commented, "Our new audit program would need to ask enough questions and test enough preventive maintenance events to be able to make recommendations on this aspect of R&M. But, let me go on with another maintenance practice called *predictive maintenance.* This uses a technique that evaluates the condition of the equipment by constant monitoring. The goal is to perform maintenance *just prior to failure*, based on the observation of the equipment. This is the time when the maintenance activity is most cost-effective and before the equipment loses performance. By doing predictive maintenance, there is little waste in the remaining life of discarded parts. Predictive maintenance has advantages over the simpler *preventive maintenance.* However, there is a cost to monitoring that must be compared to the wasted useful life of equipment and additional maintenance events in preventive maintenance. To illustrate how predictive maintenance works: Large industrial motors have big ball-bearings that become damaged over time. Bad bearings could cause catastrophic failure and burn out the motor. Using preventive maintenance, the motor would periodically be totally dismantled and the ball-bearings automatically replaced. However, with predictive maintenance, you might instead take weekly infrared pictures of the motor. It's possible to tell by observing 'hot spots' in ball-bearings, as imaged in the infrared pictures, that the motor is about to fail soon. You would then perform maintenance of the motor right away.

"To evaluate equipment condition, predictive maintenance uses nondestructive testing technologies such as infrared pictures, acoustic tests, vibration analysis, sound-level measurements, used-oil analysis, and other tests. This type of maintenance does need technical expertise that we may not have in-house."

While Matt caught his breath following this long explanation, Kirk commented, "I don't know about Trey and Chester, but we use this advanced technique in only a few plants and only on *very* selective equipment. I'm impressed that your prior R&M audit program was so sophisticated that you asked questions and had suggestions in this area. I think there are big opportunities for us with this advanced maintenance practice, but the R&M engineers throughout MultiCrown would need to be trained. Perhaps if Audit suggests this to the CEO as well . . . ?" He looked at Trey and Chester, and both signaled their agreement.

When the three engineers turned to Matt again with anticipation, he was ready this time. He'd seen the request coming. "Well, as with the new-system issue, if we can really make a case for this training, I'll gladly act as a champion. Again, we need to finish this current project first. We can't suggest much until we actually audit the R&M functions, and we can't do that until this team accomplishes its mission. However, I'm very encouraged that you see opportunities for improvement already."

Matt continued, "Let me talk a bit about a few other related topics. Good R&M departments have a set of performance metrics. For example, R&M management could measure the total hours spent on *maintenance alone*, and compare this to the total hours for *both repair and maintenance*. Eighty percent or more for maintenance hours is usually excellent. Less than 60 percent of hours dedicated to maintenance indicates the R&M process has significant opportunities. Auditors can easily calculate this to assess an R&M process. The percentage of what is best-class varies somewhat by industry, and a benchmarking effort by your team may be needed to set goals. Another good metric is to analyze the percent of planned maintenance events that are actually completed as scheduled and not postponed. Auditors can check the percent of maintenance tasks completed as originally scheduled. Over 95 percent completion rate is a good performance, as long as the missed events are completed within an established and reasonable time frame. This is the point that Chester made earlier— that some of our plants are missing the tasked scheduled maintenance. If we identified this in one of our audits, we'd try to determine the root cause of the problem, and make audit recommendations in our report."

He paused to let his comments sink in and continued, "A question for our three engineers: What types of metrics do your plants use?"

At this question, there was an uncomfortable silence, as none of the engineers wanted to admit anything too critical about their businesses. Finally, Trey hesitantly commented, "Well, I hate to say this, but we are all over the place on metrics. It is up to each individual plant, and I really don't think we use a comprehensive set of good metrics." The other two engineers nodded in a resigned manner, but didn't say anything.

Dalton observed their disturbed expressions and jumped in. "Trey, I am glad you commented on something that may be viewed as being critical of your business. I know it's not easy, but to really progress as a team, everybody will need to be able to say anything and trust the others to handle it in confidence and with sensitivity."

Matt stepped back in. "Trey, thank you for your comment; and Dalton, I appreciate the reminder about trusting each other and fully opening up. It looks like metrics will be a good area for our R&M audit program to focus on. Lots of opportunities there.

"To continue with my overview, another critical area is Spare Parts Management. For each piece of equipment, an analytic decision would need to be made as to which spare parts to stock and which should be ordered at the last minute. This depends on the criticality of the part, how expensive it is, how often it's needed, how long it takes to get the part to the plant, and so on. Again, if we found via our audits that there is little analytic work to decide on what spare parts to stock, we might issue audit recommendations."

At this, Kirk interrupted in his deep, and now loud, tone. "Now, wait a minute! Auditors aren't capable of judging our analysis on spare parts decisions!"

Meghan instantly retorted, "Why not? Our auditors have very good analytic and financial skills and they can tell when an economic analysis is comprehensive!"

Kirk came back heatedly, "How will auditors determine the frequency that a spare part is needed?"

Just before Dalton intervened to facilitate this conflict, Meghan continued, but in a deliberately gentler and calmer tone. It was obvious to Dalton and Matt that Meghan was trying hard to defuse the tense situation. "Kirk, you are, of course, right about this. I apologize for seeming to argue the point. As we initially discussed, auditors don't have technical R&M skills. What we'd do is look to see if maintenance management documented a thorough analysis of the life of the part based on hard data, and perform and document a complete and accurate cost-benefit analysis. If we saw evidence of that, we'd move on. If we saw no real investigation on the life of the part, or no cost-benefit analysis, or perhaps just a few sketchy notes, we might consider this is an area of improvement. We'd then ask many questions and test a number of parts before we'd conclude that better analysis on stocking spare parts is needed."

Reacting to Meghan's calmer and more reasonable tone, and remembering the Ground Rules, Kirk visibly calmed down as well. "Yes, I see what you mean. You'll audit our process for *determining how* we stock spare parts. You won't challenge the technical aspects, but if you don't see a thorough analysis in the files, considering all cost and technical factors, you would most likely be right that a good analysis wasn't done." Trey and Chester thoughtfully nodded at Kirk's last comment, but still seemed perturbed by what Audit might poke into. Dalton was thoroughly impressed with Meghan and began to see her in a somewhat different light.

"This has been a very useful exchange," Dalton stated, "and I'm gratified you returned to a calm level of discussion so quickly. Disagreements, if handled correctly, are healthy. They lead to better decisions. My guess is that what you just discussed about spare parts deserves a long team discussion to decide what auditors can legitimately analyze, test, and recommend."

"That's the end of my overview at this time," Matt concluded, "and I hope it set the stage for the team's effort. We have barely scratched the surface. I expect that our three engineers will be able to really flesh out the best R&M practices and processes, and then all of you could design the appropriate operational audit program for us to be able to help improve this critical area. As you can see, I firmly believe that effective R&M can greatly contribute to reducing risk, minimizing cost, and improving operations."

After waiting a minute to see if Matt was going to add anything else, Linda commented, "Matt, thank you for the overview. I can now see more clearly the types of audit recommendations we might be able to make. Let's break for the day and resume the meeting tomorrow morning at 8:00 A.M. Out first task will be to create the Team Mission Statement and then lay out the Team Milestones with target completion dates."

Dalton suggested a team dinner together to continue to get to know each other, but Linda immediately responded. "I've already made reservations at Café Istanbul down the block. Can everybody make it?" After seeing all the nods and smiles, she continued, "How about if we meet in the hotel lobby at 6:00 this evening? We can then walk to the restaurant. Before we all scatter, I want to say that I'm delighted to be working with such a talented group of professionals and I'm really looking forward to seeing what our team can accomplish." As everybody stood up to leave, there were scattered overlapping comments from the team. "Good job, Linda"; "Great start"; "Thanks for your prep, Linda"; "I'm starved!"

Matt, Dalton, and Linda stayed behind for a moment to debrief, and Dalton immediately commented, "Linda, you really did a fantastic job today. I'm very proud of you. You established quiet leadership without beating them over the head with it. The team activities so far are textbook and you're poised now to really move fast with this team."

As Dalton paused, Matt added, "Linda, I knew you had it in you. Excellent leadership today." At this lavish praise from Dalton and Matt, Linda beamed. "I *really* appreciate your help. Now, I'm ready for a Margarita! Let's see if I can find one at a Turkish restaurant."

· · ·

Just before 8:00 A.M. next morning, the team, including Dalton, was assembling in the Audit conference room. They were all very aware of the Team Ground Rule about being no more than five minutes late for team meetings, and nobody wanted to be the first to break the Ground Rules. Even Dalton had managed to get there in time! There was a background murmur from the various team members remarking on the very enjoyable dinner they shared last night. Trey was joking he didn't know that auditors liked to have fun, and Sandra was joking right back that she didn't know engineers even *knew* what fun was. Matt deliberately wasn't present for today's meeting, since on Dalton's advice, the team needed some time by itself to bond. Of course, that did not pertain to Dalton, since he was the team facilitator. On the conference table was a tray of assorted fresh muffins, provided by Lila. She well knows Matt's philosophy that food makes any meeting run better. Dalton was mentally recounting what he might have said to Sandra last night that he now may need to apologize for, "courage" spurred on by multiple adult beverages. Based on Sandra's current demeanor—smiling broadly, eyes wide, and a very bouncy walk into the conference room—he relaxed.

At 8:00 A.M. sharp, Linda, with Dalton sitting on her right, cleared her throat to signal the beginning of the meeting. "Good morning, team! I hope you all rested well last night and are ready to begin again today. I don't know about you, but I really enjoyed our time last night, and I really needed that Margarita. Kirk's volunteered to take the team minutes today and as soon as he hooks up his laptop, we can start. Thank you, Kirk. So, on our agenda this morning is creating the Team Mission Statement and beginning to lay out the Team Milestones with the relevant deliverables and the dates for Matt's review and approval. I thought if we each propose some thoughts or bullets, we can then assemble them in the right order to create our mission statement. Does anybody want to start?"

Sandra eagerly started, "Our mission is to create an R&M audit program."

Meghan quickly replied, "Wait a minute, Sandra; you're really being way too simplistic. There is a lot more to it than that."

With fiery heat, Sandra defended herself. "I'm *not* simplistic! Linda wanted bullets, and that's one of them. You can add more stuff in another bullet."

"What I meant is that your bullet is too limiting. We also want to train the auditors on how to do an R&M audit."

"That's fine," Sandra retorted with heated emotion, "but why can't you say that in another point rather than criticizing *my* suggestion?"

Linda began to panic. Everything had been running so smoothly, and all of a sudden this argument had exploded. When Linda looked at Dalton for help, he decided he'd better intervene, but wondered why this minor conversation would cause any conflict whatsoever.

"Okay, there's no need to be argumentative," Dalton commented. "This is the type of situation where if the team members really knew each other well, they could easily avoid this little misunderstanding. Meghan, I know you didn't mean to, but the way you worded your comment you implied that Sandra *herself* is simplistic. We all realize you didn't mean it that way, but many times, what we mean is *not* what's heard. You could have just suggested another bullet that the mission includes training the auditors, without criticizing what Sandra suggested."

"Sandra, you also became defensive too fast. You could have given Meghan a break and assumed that her heart was in the right place, but that she just didn't word her comment in the most diplomatic manner. Especially in the team Forming stage, and as you move into the Storming stage, you'll all need to be very careful as to how you express your disagreements so that you don't insult each other. Be extra diplomatic! At the same time, please try not to get bent out of shape over any one comment. If a pattern is emerging and you feel you need to clear the air with somebody, you can meet privately and explain why you're upset. Don't say, 'You're insulting me'; instead say, 'When you did this, I felt insulted, or I thought I was insulted.' It's a better way to express why you're upset without putting the other person on the defensive."

Both Sandra and Meghan looked abashed, but Meghan was the first to quietly comment. "I'm really sorry, Sandra. I got too excited and spoke without thinking it through. Of course, I don't mean *you* are simple; I just wanted to add some more content to our mission. You and Dalton were right that I should have just suggested another bullet of my own to the mission statement."

Sandra, in a somber voice, ruefully replied, "I'm sorry I got defensive, too; I have six older brothers, and I always felt attacked when I was growing up. I've been trying to not react so *energetically* when somebody disagrees with me."

Meghan replied, trying to lighten the mood, "Sandra, believe me, the *last* thing I want to do is insult an Olympic fencing champion who grew up in a house full of knife throwers. Also, I have four brothers myself—I know what you mean!" At this, Sandra chuckled and they both looked to Linda to move them past this point.

Dalton and Linda briefly exchanged a knowing look. Both were pleased that Meghan had the maturity, skills, and humor to get herself out of trouble and reestablish constructive relations with Sandra.

Relieved that the immediate conflict seemed to have passed, Linda looked around to the rest of the team. They had stayed quiet, not knowing what to do about Sandra and Meghan, but she saw them nodding when Dalton was providing advice, and perhaps the snippy exchange was good for the team in the long run. "Okay, then," Linda asked in a neutral tone, "other bullets?"

Kirk spoke up, "How about if the mission statement has a sentence or two explaining why an effective R&M audit program is needed or is valuable?"

"Good," Linda replied. "Let's get it on the list."

"Maybe a sentence or two that addresses how we'll know if the R&M audit program is successful? I'm not quite sure how to do this myself, but maybe some of you have ideas," Trey suggested.

Chester offered, "Well, how about if for the first three R&M audits, all the audit observations and suggestions would be reviewed by a panel of R&M engineers to vet them for accuracy and value?"

The three engineers turned to look at the auditors, waiting for a reaction to this unusual suggestion. After taking a long moment to carefully consider how to word her response, Meghan, in a deliberately calm tone, replied, "It's a very good idea to have a panel of R&M experts review our audit observations and suggestions for the first few audits. This would give us feedback that the R&M audit program is working as designed, and our audit points are valid and have value. However, we need to be careful to maintain the professional audit standard that calls for us to have the independence to make recommendations without undue interference. I'm pretty sure we can work this out so that the panel of engineers might make comments on our audit points, but ultimately it would be our decision as to what to include in our audit reports. Of course, we want to be reasonable and make responsible suggestions, so we are very likely to listen to the advice of our R&M experts. I think this one is a policy issue where we'll need Matt's approval."

Kirk, Chester, and Trey all nodded their appreciation that this would be a very extraordinary step for Internal Audit, and were happy that Meghan was seriously considering the suggestion. The body language of all the team members seemed to indicate that everyone was impressed at how Meghan handled such a potential issue in a calm, constructive manner.

For the next couple of hours, the team continued to generate ideas and explore various aspects of their mission. Eventually, they reached a time when no further suggestions were forthcoming. At one point during the morning, Dalton reminded the team that fully agreeing to a clear and comprehensive mission statement would keep them out of trouble later on. By having their mission statement visible during all meetings, they would reduce the risk of veering off in the wrong direction. Finally, at about 11:30 A.M., Linda suggested they go out and grab some Chinese food. Meghan begged off that she was on a diet and had brought some raw vegetable to eat for lunch. Dalton always had to laugh to himself at the women in great shape who were on a diet. However, he was wise enough to never voice this thought out loud. Meghan volunteered that during lunch, she would work to put all the bullets into a coherent mission statement that the team could review when they got back.

Linda responded to Meghan's offer with an effusive, "Thank you, that's great of you! We'll see you in about an hour. Let me stop by Matt's office and ask if he wants to join us for lunch. It's a Szechuan restaurant, and I know Matt likes spicy food. Of course, he likes *all* foods!"

Meghan sat with her depressing bag of lonely, raw vegetables and munched loudly as she drafted the Team Mission Statement on the laptop. After about 45 minutes, she looked up with satisfaction at the mission statement projected on the screen. She wished she were as satisfied with her raw vegetables, and sorry she'd missed out on the Chinese food with the others.

R&M/Audit Team Mission Statement

MultiCrown spends over $800 million annually on Repair and Maintenance. The R&M processes, systems, and practices vary significantly across MultiCrown's divisions, and even at different plants within divisions. The variability in R&M performance across the plants indicates significant opportunities for improvement if all the plants could operate at the level of the best MultiCrown R&M functions.

An excellent R&M function greatly reduces capital expenditures. Properly maintained equipment reduces the chances of expensive loss of production due to failure of critical equipment. Well-maintained equipment also helps meet quality standards and contributes to customer satisfaction. It is much more cost-effective to maintain equipment than to repair it once broken.

The R&M/Audit Team is charged with creating a full-fledged, comprehensive internal audit discipline with the objective to systematically assess and recommend improvements to MultiCrown's R&M functions across all global businesses. The audit discipline is to include an audit and testing program, a reference guide that can support auditors as they execute the audit steps, and a specific training program on R&M best practices that is provided to the entire audit staff.

The team will also create a communications plan that will be used to explain the new R&M audit discipline to all MultiCrown business leaders and R&M managers.

• • •

All the team members had returned from lunch and were thoughtfully analyzing Meghan's summary. After a few moments, Linda commented. "Meghan, this is a great job. Thank you so much for doing this while we were out."

Meghan replied, "No problem, Linda. It's actually pretty hard to write something as a team; it's much easier for one person to do so and then the rest can take shots at it. The way we did it, using all of our suggested bullets, I was able to quickly assemble them into a full-fledged mission statement. I just noticed I didn't include a way to assess the success of the R&M audit discipline we develop. I think we need to add this to complete the mission statement. Don't we, Dalton?"

"Yes, we definitely should add this," Dalton concurred. "With a typical problem-solving team, the measure of success is usually something very quantifiable about the process itself. For example, reduce errors by 30 percent, or improve throughput by 20 percent, or reduce by half the hours needed to execute a process. With a product development team, such as ours, the measure of success is harder to figure out, and not as readily quantifiable. So put yourselves six months in the future. Your team's mission has been completed, and you've been doing R&M audits. How would you know if the team has succeeded and the R&M audit recommendations are valuable to MultiCrown?"

They were all silent for several minutes while they thought. Sandra finally said, "Well, since Matt is our sponsor, if he is satisfied with the results, then our team succeeded."

Meghan, aware of the prior conflict between them, very carefully replied. "We certainly need to have Matt be satisfied with our results. For one thing, he's our boss and does our performance evaluations! However, is this enough? If Matt is satisfied, would this mean that our team succeeded? Would the R&M people call this a success just because Matt's happy with the results?"

"Our R&M people would be pleased with this audit effort if it resulted in *real* improvements to our R&M shops," Chester immediately retorted. "For example, if we get a new system out of it, or if we get the additional training needed for predictive maintenance, or if the audit recommendations are valuable."

Linda replied, "Well, as Matt said, the new system and new training are possible further efforts following our current team mission. I don't think it would be fair to judge our team by those criteria, since further analysis will need to be done."

Chester continued, "That's true, but how about judging the *value* and *validity* of the audit recommendations? We could use the R&M expert panel we mentioned earlier to review all the audit recommendations from the first three R&M audits and determine if the R&M/Audit team has succeeded."

Meghan, after several moments to digest this suggestion, slowly commented, "As we mentioned earlier, we really need Matt's approval for this review panel and we need to make sure that auditor independence isn't affected. Can I get on the computer and draft a further sentence to our mission statement draft? Matt will need to approve the entire mission statement, anyway, so he can decide on the engineers' panel at the time."

Meghan then typed at the bottom of the mission statement draft:

> In order to determine the success of the R&M/Audit team, a panel of five R&M engineers will evaluate every audit recommendation for the first three R&M audits. For each recommendation, they will assess if the recommendation is both valid and value-adding. If 90 percent of the recommendations are approved by the majority of the panel (three or more engineers out of five), then the R&M Audit Program can be deemed to be successful.

The team members all looked at this addition for a long time before Linda commented, "Meghan, I think you really captured it. I'm not sure about the 90 percent—that seems to be a very high threshold."

Sandra jumped in, "I like it. This gives us something pretty concrete to use to evaluate our team. Of course, it's still based on the subjective assessment of the panel, but it may be the best we can do for our kind of team."

Linda turned to the three engineers and asked, "What do you all think?" While all three nodded enthusiastically, Kirk commented, "I think this would work. I do believe the panel will need to devote effort to determine what are 'value-adding' and 'valid' audit recommendations, but I'm sure we can come up with some type of point scale."

At this point, Dalton stood up. "Team, it has been real, but I've got a dinner engagement I need to leave for and some work to do beforehand. How about if you all sleep on it, and we can revisit the mission statement tomorrow morning? If we still like it in the morning, Linda can drag Matt in so he can approve it and we can go on with developing the Team Milestones." Dalton failed to mention that his dinner was with Sandra and he wanted to make sure he had plenty of time to get ready, especially given the phone calls he had to return first. He definitely wanted to shave his head to make it, as his daughter would say, smooth as a baby's tush.

"I think it's a good idea to break at this time," Linda replied. "However, I'm not sure about the '*dragging* Matt in' part. Would it be okay if I *politely* ask him if he could join us?" Her plaintive tone brought laughter from around the table.

As they started packing up their things, Linda asked, "Who is up for Italian food tonight?" Several team members left the conference room discussing where and when to meet for dinner, but Sandra ducked out pretty fast. She wanted to get ready for her rendezvous with Dalton.

. . .

It was 8:00 A.M., Thursday morning. The entire team was at the conference room on time, including a bleary-eyed Dalton. Dalton and Sandra conspicuously walked in together, speaking quietly and laughing. They were all somewhat tired after a late night, but at least they had the coffee and donuts Lila had brought in.

Linda started, "Good morning, team!" Even though the other team members mostly grumbled as they waited for more coffee to hit their system, Linda continued in an annoyingly bubbly tone. "I hope you all slept well. Sandra volunteered to take the minutes today—thank you, Sandra!"

"Let's start out with our draft Team Mission Statement. What do you all think of it this morning?" They all stared at the screen with the projected statement. "We really need to have this as a full consensus of the team before asking Matt for his approval. How about this? Does anybody have any objections or anything else to add? Remember, we don't want Groupthink here." After a quiet moment without comments and with thoughtful nods all around, Linda continued, "Okay, just to make sure, let's go around the room and each of you say either 'yea' or 'nay.' Dalton, as we agreed, you don't get a formal vote, but please let us know if you have any suggestions before we vote."

Dalton had nothing to add; and after another minute, with all "yea" responses, the team formally agreed to propose the mission statement to Matt. Linda left the conference room and came back in a few minutes with Matt. She was glad she had given him a heads-up last night that they might need his approval this morning.

Matt sat down with a cheery, "Good morning, team! Linda explained you want me to approve the Team Mission Statement." He grabbed a chocolate donut and without saying anything further, Matt read, then reread, then rereread the mission statement on the screen. In a very thoughtful tone, Matt commented, "You all did a great job. The mission statement includes why R&M is significant and important to MultiCrown's success; why there's a gap and why we should help improve the R&M processes across the board; what the team plans to deliver; and, finally, how we'll know if the team succeeds. I think it's complete, concise, and comprehensive. We'll need to give some more thought as to how the R&M engineers' review panel will work, but that can be done later. I do need to emphasize that we in Internal Audit must be the ones who decide what is included in our audit reports. The panel can advise us on the validity and value-adding nature of our recommendations, but ultimately it will be our decision. I formally approve the Team Mission Statement!"

Clearing her throat loudly, Linda got everyone's attention. "Matt, thank you for your approval. For the rest of the day and probably into the next video meeting or two, we'll be working to lay out the milestones with the delivery dates, define the various project modules, assign tasks to team members, and generally lay out the detailed portion of our development. Our intent is to get your approval again after these things are done so we know we're going in the right direction."

"Sure! Good plan," Matt said. "I'll be tied up most of the day and probably won't see you before you fly back this afternoon. I think this will be a valuable program for MultiCrown. I really do want to thank all of you, but especially our engineer friends for joining us on this effort. Maybe after we are all done, we can make you three honorary auditors!"

The engineers grimaced in mock horror at this offer, but it was Chester who carefully said, "That would *indeed* be *quite* an honor; however, I'm not sure we could live up to such high moral standards!" Given his dry, fake-British tone, the entire team burst into laughter.

Once the chuckles died down, Matt turned to Sandra, "I'm glad you're staying an extra day. Can we meet tomorrow morning to discuss the current business situation in South America and your upcoming audits?" Following Sandra's quick "Sure," Matt stood up, shook hands with the three engineers, and left the team to continue their morning's work.

When they'd all returned from lunch, Linda began by asking Dalton, "Where do you think we are in the stages of teaming?" It was obvious to Dalton the entire team had already discussed this and now wanted validation from him.

He replied, "You're doing great. I think the careful, deliberate launch helped you get through the Forming stage very quickly. We had some *Storming events*, but really pretty mild compared to most teams I have worked with. You all resolved these conflicts very quickly. I'd say you're now in the early Norming stage and, hopefully, you'll soon be entering the Performing stage. Something to remember is that most teams meet a couple of hours a week. By your meeting for almost three straight days to start out, plus having several meals together, you now have the equivalent of about 10 or 12 *regular* meetings under your belt.

"The formal Ground Rules helped you. The thorough introductions helped. Having a team sponsor with a very clear idea of what he wants *really* helped.

Linda, you have done a wonderful job leading the team. I think the team members of this team really fit very well together and you all have a high degree of maturity and interpersonal skills. Of course, my facilitation was *magnificent!*" He tried to keep a straight face, but cracked up as he said this. Dalton was always very appreciative of his own humor. He continued, "Seriously, I'm very impressed with how fast and smoothly you all created your mission statement and reached consensus on it, and how well you're progressing with your Milestones and team assignments. Some teams in the Storming stage can really get stuck at this point.

"I need to leave for another meeting, but Kirk, Chester, and Trey, it was great to meet you and I hope you have smooth flights home. I'm looking forward to working with all of you soon." He stood up and shook hands all around, including a more lingering handshake with Sandra. This he accompanied with a discreet wink. He was glad they had arranged another quiet dinner together that night.

At this point, everybody was standing up and packing their things to leave. Linda almost hugged the engineers, but at the last moment decided it might seem more natural when the team was in the Performing stage. Also, she didn't know how they might feel about being hugged by an *auditor*! With positive words about the meeting and working together, they all walked out of the conference room.

People-Centric Skills Highlighted in This Chapter

Stages of Team Development*

Psychologist Bruce Tuckman, PhD, was requested by his boss at the Naval Medical Research Institute, Bethesda, MD, to review 50 articles about team behavior. From this body of work, Dr. Tuckman conceived his theory of group developmental processes in 1965. This theory states that there are four distinct stages of team development: the Forming stage, the Storming stage, the Norming stage, and the Performing stage.

All successful teams need to move through all four stages in sequence, although it is possible for a team to retrograde to the Storming stage if there are unexpected changes in the mission, or if new team

---

*M. K. Smith, "Bruce W. Tuckman: Forming, Storming, Norming and Performing in Groups," *Encyclopedia of Informal Education*, 2005.

members need to be added later in the life of the team. The faster a team moves though the first three stages, the faster it reaches its most productive condition, the Performing stage.

Forming Stage

When a new team forms, the initial concerns for the team members center on getting to know each other and beginning to understand the purpose of the team. Since the team members do not know each other well, they tend to act independently and full trust is generally not possible. Team members' behavior is driven by a desire to be accepted by the others and avoiding conflict. Individuals are also gathering information and impressions about each other, and about the scope of the task and how to approach it. The members are establishing relationships with the team leader, team sponsor, and fellow team members.

In the Forming stage, the leader's role is critical and strong leadership skills are essential. Leaders have to provide a safe and constructive environment for a healthy rapport among the team members and to establish a sound foundation to accomplish the mission.

Storming Stage

The second stage is characterized by conflict and polarization around interpersonal issues. Team members open up to each other and opinions are tested and challenged. In the Storming phase, the team members begin to address the team objectives, suggesting ideas and possible paths. Very different ideas and approaches may compete for consideration; and, if badly managed, this phase can be destructive for the team. Some team members may try to become dominant over other team members.

The maturity of team members, and the extent of their People-Centric Skills, usually determine whether the team will move out of this stage. It can be contentious, unpleasant, and even painful to team members who are averse to conflict. Tolerance of each team member and their differences should be emphasized. In the Storming stage, the team leader must address conflict head-on. Team conflict is normal in this phase, and helps spark creativity. Clear and honest communication is important during this phase of the group's journey. It is also important to help team members continue to build trust. Trust is built through transparent behavior and communication.

Several team activities can shorten the time spent in the Storming stage. A very comprehensive session to introduce the team members to each other will be helpful, as interpersonal understanding helps build

(continued)

trust. Sharing meals and numerous different types of team-building activities is conducive to the team members getting to know each other as individuals. Another early key activity for the team is to create a good set of Team Ground Rules. This sets the stage for expected and acceptable behavior by the team members and minimizes certain types of conflict. Finally, jointly creating a very clear Team Mission Statement helps the team by providing clarity as to what it is to accomplish. This also reduces conflict between personal interests and team goals.

Norming Stage

The resistance and conflict that was prevalent during the Storming stage is generally overcome in the Norming stage. Roles and Mission have been set, and people are now beginning to work on their tasks. Teams begin agreeing on the rules and values by which they operate. In the ideal situation, teams begin to trust themselves and each other during this phase as they accept the vital contributions of each member toward achieving the team's goals.

In this stage, honest, personal opinions can be safely expressed by team members, and they have trust their fellow team members will listen to them and carefully consider their ideas and contributions. Teams must watch out for Groupthink here. Following the turbulent Storming stage, team members may give in too fast to avoid a recurrence of the recent painful conflicts. It is important team members know that they must express their full opinions for the good of the team, even if they do word their opinions in a careful and diplomatic manner.

As individual members take greater responsibility during this stage, the team leader can take a step back from the leadership role.

Performing Stage

The final period for the team is the Performing stage. By now, the team should be well into their work and significant progress made on their objectives. Communication is clear and direct. Team members are sharing knowledge and working well together.

Once teams move from Norming to Performing, they can be identified by high levels of independence, motivation, knowledge, and competence. Decision making is collaborative, and dissent is expected and encouraged as there will be a high level of respect in the communication between team members. Consensus is smoothly and quickly reached.

Since the team is functioning in a highly independent way in the Performing phase, the team leader shifts partially into a support and mentoring role to provide task or process resources to help the team complete its objectives.

Team Ground Rules

The Team Ground Rules are guidelines that help the team members manage their group behavior. Setting up the rules very early in team's formation helps prevent some problems before they begin. Many ground rules deal with how to treat each other as team members, but also include basic rules about behavior of the team, such as deadlines, punctuality, and meeting commitments on assigned tasks. Although there are many areas that can be covered when formulating these rules, the team will run smoother when everyone knows what they can and cannot do. Good Ground Rules help a team progress much faster through the early stages of team development and are particularly useful to get past the conflict-ridden Storming stage to the more productive Norming and Performing stages.

Examples of Team Ground Rules

- Team meetings: frequency, location, day/time of the week or month, length of meetings.
- In-person meetings vs. virtual meetings (videoconference or telephone conference call).
- If video or phone conference, method and arrangements.
- Priority of team meetings over other time demands for team members. If possible, establish the team meetings as very high priority for the team members. The managers of the team members may need to be included in this decision.
- Team decision-making process. For example: Strategic decisions, by team sponsor with team recommendation. Important decisions, by team consensus. Procedural decisions, by simple vote unless someone objects (if so, then discuss and work toward consensus).
- Agreement as to team member punctuality for team meetings.
- Assignment of minutes-taker for each meeting. This role may rotate among team members, except for the team leader, who will be focused on keeping the meetings running smoothly.
- Location of and access to team documents.
- How team documents can be updated, viewed, and edited by team members.
- Assignments should be provided to the full team 24–48 hours before the meeting when the results will be discussed.

(continued)

■ Specific project milestone dates will be established for key deliverables.

■ Milestone deliverables to be formally approved by the team sponsor before the team progresses further.

■ Conversations or opinions stated during team meetings will not be shared with anyone outside the team unless approved by the team. This is essential to encourage full honesty and maintain trust.

Team Mission Statement

A Team Mission Statement is usually made up of a few short paragraphs that identify the goals and objectives of the team. The mission statement is usually the first real collaborative effort by the team. It is a way of promoting a discussion that focuses a team's activities and keeps the members on track for achieving their objective. It helps to concisely clarify for each team member why the team was formed and what it needs to accomplish. The mission statement should be displayed or available at each team meeting, and should be periodically reviewed by the team to make any revisions deemed necessary. Commitment to a common mission improves teamwork and helps avoid needless conflicts that lack of clarity might foster.

The Team Mission Statement is also a mechanism for communicating with the team sponsor(s) to ensure there is full agreement as to what the team is charged to do. It is valuable to have the sponsor(s) formally approve the Team Mission Statement and any subsequent revisions.

The Team Mission Statement is usually made up of several components and addresses several key questions, including: Why is the subject for the team significant and important to the organization's success? What is the gap between the current situation and the desired situation? (If possible, this gap should be quantified with metrics.) What should the team create or improve to close the gap between the current and desired situation? What form will the team output take? (For example: reports, recommendations, process changes, new process, etc.) Finally, how will the team and the sponsor know if the team is successful? If metrics were able to be established for defining the process gap, then the metrics before and after the team results are implemented can help validate the team's success. If the desired results were not fully met, perhaps a Phase Two may be needed by the team, or a new team with different skills may be needed.

Consensus Building

Building consensus is an important skill for teams. *Consensus* is the point of maximum agreement on a team decision. A consensus decision does not mean it is the preferred decision for every team member or even for any one member; it is the best decision that everyone can agree to and support. It is a situation in which everyone feels that he or she has one solution that does not compromise any strong personal convictions or individual needs.

To reach consensus, group members discuss, evaluate, and prioritize ideas, and struggle to reach the best conclusions together. It requires a high level of interpersonal maturity by team members so they know what is truly important to them and to the team overall. It also means that team members must be willing to compromise on appropriate points to reach the best decision for the entire team. Each team member must understand the points where there is no give at all, and the points that could be changed to reach a consensus decision. If team members are too inflexible about noncritical items, a consensus might never be reached. Everyone on the team needs to discuss and understand the general nature of reaching consensus before an actual attempt is made at a real team decision.

A team facilitator, who has no stake in the team tasks, may be useful to objectively drive the consensus process. Sometimes a discussion with the team sponsor may be needed to help break a stalemate within the team.

CHAPTER SEVEN

7

Communicating to Build Relationships

People-Centric Skills

Relationship Building; Promoting the Role of Internal Audit; Optimized Listening Skills; Active Listening; Building Trust; Nonverbal Communications

MATT WALKED QUICKLY back to his office after meeting with the CEO. Caleb had wanted to tell him, in person, that he asked Tom Peterson to leave MultiCrown. While Matt was somewhat surprised that Caleb wanted to communicate this privately, he wasn't shocked at the decision to fire Tom. Head of the Plastics Molding Division, Tom Peterson, was being officially "retired" by the Company. It was regarded as early, elective retirement, but most executives and experienced employees would know better. Tom was being pushed out, mainly due to the lackluster performance of his Division over the past three years. Out of the five MultiCrown divisions, the Plastics Molding Division had significantly lagged behind the rest of the Company, and all major competitors, in revenue and profit margin. Not only that, the fraud that had been uncovered by Matt's team played a part as well. Caleb specifically emphasized to Matt that the weak financial and operational controls in the Division highlighted a lack of discipline that not only led to the poor performance, but probably permitted the fraud to occur. He also noted that he had been increasingly concerned by Tom's lack of support for the MultiCrown corporate culture. This was the only division where the attitude toward fraud, and controls in general, seemed passive, and that was definitely not Caleb's point of view.

The main reason Caleb wanted a discussion with Matt was that the Division really needed to greatly improve its culture and tone-at-the-top, including the rest of the internal control environment. Caleb asked if the Audit Plan could be adjusted so the auditors could spend more time helping the new head of the Division. The new leader needed to have an independent view of the controls and process opportunities; and, in Caleb's view, Tom's existing team was suspect, since Tom had selected most of them.

Matt had immediately agreed to this request from Caleb. He reassured him that whenever a new leader came aboard, he emphasized building a trusting relationship, essentially "marketing" or promoting the positive aspects that Internal Audit can bring to the table.

Based on their long history of conflicts, Matt had not respected Tom much over the years he had known him, nor did he believe he was a good leader. The auditors had many run-ins with Tom, especially in his role as divisional president. However, since the last audit, where significant issues were uncovered, including the emerging fraud, Tom's opinion of Matt and the auditors *had* begun to change somewhat. Tom seemed to have a newfound respect for Matt and his team, and had worked diligently to address the issues that were identified in the audit report. However, Matt somewhat cynically thought that maybe Tom was driven by fear of losing his job.

Matt had spent some time with Tom since the last audit, and their mutual love of cooking had fostered a connection that Matt did not believe possible a few months ago. Matt felt bad for Tom, since he had given many years to MultiCrown, but also realized this was probably the best decision for the Company. If only Tom would have trusted him and Internal Audit a few years earlier, he might have been able to improve his controls and operational performance, and perhaps avoided the "early retirement."

Caleb had informed him that they had decided to go outside the Company to find Tom's replacement. The Division needed a fresh perspective. MultiCrown had snagged the second in command at their largest plastics molding competitor, PetroChem. Karl Saint was a relatively young man, but very accomplished. He was credited with many of the innovations at PetroChem that had brought them from a medium-sized player to a major competitor. According to Caleb, Karl was starting next week and he asked Matt to establish a strong personal rapport with him right from the start. Matt assured him that this was a standard practice whenever a key leader was hired. He would call Karl immediately to welcome him to MultiCrown, and to offer Audit's help with the transition.

As Matt briefly chatted with Lila about his day's schedule, he thought about how the Internal Audit Outreach program he had developed over many years could be improved. Matt had always been a proponent of actively promoting internal audit, but he believed that he might need a new perspective on this topic, as his program might have grown a bit out of date.

Late that afternoon, Matt gave Dalton a quick call to pick his brain. "Matt, great to hear from you! I'm in Dallas. I just conducted a class on leadership skills, and I'm spending some time catching up with potential clients. Right now I'm in my hotel room going through my mountain of email. How's everything on your end?"

"Dalton, things are very good. Everything's progressing nicely with the audit team. I just wanted to spend a few minutes catching up and also to bend your ear on a new project. Meghan continues to make great progress. I know she has reached out to you for advice, and I appreciate your being there for her. She's spoken very highly of the assistance you've given her." If Matt could have seen Dalton's face at this moment, he would note the huge grin, as Dalton and Meghan had developed a *very* good friendship.

Matt continued, "I did want to let you know that Tom Peterson is taking early retirement. This is still confidential, but I did want to keep you in the loop, especially since I'm asking for your help. We've tapped someone named Karl Saint from PetroChem to lead the Division. I'm excited about this and I want your help in brainstorming ideas to continue to promote Internal Audit inside MultiCrown. I want to make sure that we capitalize on this change and establish strong rapport with the new division head. Can we schedule some time for us to sit down with the team and brainstorm improvements to our Audit Outreach strategy? We implemented one internally years ago, but I feel like it might be a bit stale and I would love a new perspective. Also, I hope you'll have some suggestions you can share with us on how to establish a good solid business relationship with a key person. New leaders are constantly joining MultiCrown, and setting a good foundation for us to work together would be great. This seems to me to be a People-Centric skill."

Dalton, always known to speak with excitement in his voice, seemed a little more wound up than normal. "Matt, thank you so much for reaching out and giving me this opportunity to work with your team again! I love the concept of a formal process to promote Internal Audit, and don't believe that enough audit executives take this proactive approach. Let me know what date works best for you and we will make it happen. However, I must ask, did Tom *really* retire?"

"Well, that's the *official* story," Matt replied. "However, you know the many past operational and control problems of his division and its poor financial performance since Tom took over. It wouldn't surprise me if these factors had something to do with Tom's *retirement*." Matt felt a bit uncomfortable not telling Dalton the entire story, but his discussion with Caleb was confidential. However, he knew with Dalton's organizational savvy that he well understood what had not been explicitly said.

"Okay, Dalton, let's work our schedule, and Lila will get back to you with some possible dates. Catch you later!"

"Sure, buddy. I am always open to discuss 'dates' with Lila!" He chuckled in self-appreciation as he hung up the phone.

Lila scheduled a working session for the afternoon of the 14th. In many cases, for this level of discussion, Matt would include his direct reports. This time, Matt decided to include not only himself and Dalton, but also Meghan and Jim, his two directors, as well as Linda. Matt wanted to continue to watch Meghan's progress, but also to give Jim an opportunity to redeem himself after he continued to reject the value of improving his communications and interpersonal skills. Also, Jim's supervision of Linda, his IT Audit Manager, had continued to deteriorate. Matt saw Linda continuing to shine and grow as she capably led the R&M Audit Development Team. He also saw the benefits of the great mentoring relationship between Meghan and Linda. But the fact that Linda couldn't look to Jim, her immediate supervisor, for assistance was indicative of a very bad relationship. This might be Jim's last chance to turn the corner.

● ● ●

Dalton didn't mind traveling; it was in the nature of what he did for a living. However, it did become overwhelming at times. With his vocation, he was able to visit wonderful cities throughout the world. The irony was that they all were blending together: airport–hotel–conference center–airport. In addition, with his kids at a young age, he was always in a hurry to get home.

The one significant advantage to being a world traveler and racking up many frequent flyer miles was upgrading to first class. First-class travel has changed over the years, but you could always count on a few advantages: a nice, large, relatively comfortable seat, a meal (well, at least *some* food), and a cocktail to relax. Flying back to Chicago, Dalton ordered a Bloody Mary and began to think through the conversation he'd had with Matt. Promoting Internal Audit is something that every audit department should do, but it was not viewed as a high priority. With the nature of internal auditing continuing to evolve away from being the "police" or strictly focusing on compliance and assurance, the need to educate the organization on the benefits and role of internal auditing continued to take on more importance. The key to showing "value" was to continue to demonstrate Audit's contributions and build significant trust. Marketing, or promoting, Internal Audit should start at the top but also cascade down to all levels, he believed. Dalton learned, through building his business and Internal Audit departments from the ground up, that all relationships are meaningful, regardless of what level the person is. People need to learn the importance of Internal Audit early in their careers, so they can carry that forward as they continue to progress in their careers.

Dalton opened his laptop and began to compile a list of steps to effectively promote internal audit:

- Building effective relationships with Employees (key attributes include)
  - Transparency
  - Trust
  - Active listening
  - Continuous communication
- Establishing relationships with Management, including
  - Periodic (quarterly) meetings with management
  - Regularly scheduled lunches with key personnel
  - Introductory meetings with new management
  - One-page summary of the benefits of internal audit
- Educating the Organization, including
  - Brown-bag educational lunch sessions
  - Newsletters
  - Training sessions
  - Audit website

Dalton began to think about the reasons why some people didn't like internal auditors. Unfortunately, the word *audit* had an inherently negative connotation and many people think of an auditor as someone who is out to get them. One of the most important roles of effectively promoting Internal Audit is getting the organization past the preconceived notions of the term *auditor*. A challenge for audit departments was to convince management that Audit is actually trying to help protect them while trying to improve the organization;

the goal of audit is not to play *gotcha!* A good outreach or communications plan for Internal Audit needs to clearly explain the true role of audit. With strong interpersonal and communication skills, internal auditors could alleviate the inherent fear of their job title and begin to build strong relationships. Additionally, with increased transparency, auditors can build trust and a more effective Internal Audit process.

As Dalton began to update and create an outline for Matt to review, the flight attendant announced that the plane was beginning to descend. Dalton was excited about being home again and pleased with the progress he had made on the plane—more progress in the air, less work to do at home, and more time to spend with the kids.

• • •

Just after lunch, Matt settled in the conference room with a fresh cup of coffee and his laptop. It was a few minutes before 1:00 and he wanted to catch up on email prior to the start of the meeting with the team and Dalton. Email can be quite overwhelming at times. There were many different theories on how to keep up with email; many try to have times during the day when they check email. Matt, on the other hand, took the opposite approach. He tried to answer each important email in real time as they were received. He had the same real-time theory on email as Dalton did. Matt believed greatly in the customer service aspect of Internal Audit and wanted to make sure he was responsive to the needs of his staff and MultiCrown management. His goal was always to respond within 24 hours; it was definitely an ambitious goal. It seemed like every time he started to make progress, he was interrupted. With that thought barely formed, Meghan walked in for the meeting.

Lately, Meghan seemed to be very self-possessed, and happy. Ever since Matt had started to mentor her, the strides she had made were apparent. She was more open and confident and did not micromanage her team. She seemed to take pleasure in finding valid reasons to compliment the auditors and encourage them to continue to do excellent work. The auditors also had seen the welcome changes in Meghan and now were strong supporters. Matt and Dalton's advice had greatly helped Meghan in turning the corner. But this happiness seemed to be deeper than just work-related. When Matt engaged her in small-talk, she tended to bring up Dalton fairly frequently. She seemed to have a natural glow. Every time she mentioned his name, you could see her eyebrows twitch ever so slightly. Additionally, she had a very faint smile in the corners of her mouth. Matt had picked up many tips on facial recognition and reading gesture clusters from Dalton. He was starting to see the usefulness.

Matt didn't even notice when Jim entered the room quietly, accompanied by Linda. Jim, as IT Audit Director, had not embraced the enhanced P-C skills focus that Matt and Dalton had brought to the audit team. Matt had continued to have issues with him, and the gap between them seemed to be inevitably widening. Additionally, Matt had taken an increased interest in Linda's professional development, and he felt Jim's management style was hurting her growth. Jim, not adept at expressing his feelings constructively, didn't broach this subject with Matt, but Matt's obvious support for Linda, at his expense, was very upsetting.

Jim had always seemed to be uncomfortable in group settings, and with the issues he was having, he often retreated into his introverted shell. Linda, after being promoted to Manager the previous year, continued to grow into her role. Jim was not pleased with Linda, as she didn't seem to listen to his guidance, and took a very different approach to auditing. Linda was very focused on building relationships with auditees and spending a significant amount of time face-to-face with them. Jim, on the other hand, felt that establishing such close relationships was an independence issue, and preferred to focus on analyzing the data and assessing compliance with process controls. This difference in orientation continued to drive a wedge between them.

Dalton sauntered in, casually late, with an extra bounce in his step. Matt noticed a new three-piece suit with maroon-checked shirt and sky-blue-and-crimson tie. Finally, Matt noticed new black-and-white wingtip shoes. Not many people can pull those shoes off, thought Matt, but Dalton made the flashy fashion statement look professional. Matt observed Meghan taking in a full head-to-toe look at Dalton, and saw her appreciative smile. Uncharacteristically, she was also twirling her hair—this certainly *seemed* flirtatious. He didn't need Dalton to interpret *that* one!

After everyone was settled, Matt kicked off the team meeting. "Thank you, all, for your time. As I conveyed via the meeting notice, I wanted to get you together to discuss updating the Internal Audit Outreach plan. What we have used in the past has worked, but I think it needs to be refreshed, and I'm looking for some new ideas. I would first like to ask for your suggestions. Thoughts, anyone?"

Meghan chimed in confidently. "Matt, I love that we are focusing on this, and there are a few things I'd like to propose right off the bat. One, how about a brown-bag monthly luncheon where we try to communicate or explain a different aspect or service of Audit to the organization? If we can afford it, maybe we even buy lunch for the attendees to pull in the crowd? Everyone loves a free lunch! We should also probably expand on our quarterly 'checkpoint' meetings with management, where we try to continue to understand their key risks, new opportunities, additional challenges, and changes in their organization. We can use these meetings to also explain what else we might be able to help them with."

As Meghan spoke, Dalton continued to read Jim's sullen and obviously angry body language. He rolled his eyes and postured away from Meghan at the conference table. He continued to tap his foot throughout her speech and did not seem engaged whatsoever. Matt was trying to keep his cool, but Dalton knew Jim was grating on Matt's last nerve. However, at the opposite end of the spectrum, was Linda. She listened intently, took copious notes, nodded her head approvingly on a few occasions, and looked to Matt to continue.

"Meghan, very good ideas and a great start! We really need to put together a calendar of brown-bag lunches and post it months in advance to make sure people can plan around it. I think we can spring for lunch for the first few sessions. I agree that we should expand on our 'checkpoints' and discuss who else should be involved. Jim, anything to add?" Matt tried to make this last comment sound positive, but there was a tinge of sarcasm to it.

With some reluctance, Jim commented, "Matt, to be completely honest, I wish this 'marketing' stuff would work, but I don't think it's an effective use of our time! Let's go in, get our job done, not shove the work down on them, but if we get a ton of resistance, know when to push or pull and just get the work done! I think we spend way too much time with this fluffy stuff and not doing the work!" Jim had become passionate here, as was apparent in his louder, more strident tone of voice.

Looking back, this moment appeared to be the straw that broke the camel's back for Matt. He had great posture and did not give up too much through body language, but Dalton was able to read him like a book during Jim's last comment. Instead of acting perturbed or hunching his shoulders and appearing deflated, Matt gave away nothing to Jim. In fact, he almost appeared calm at this last comment. "Jim, thank you for your comments; I guess we are going to have to agree to disagree on that." Dalton had recognized this before; it was Matt's very subtle sign that he was done putting more effort and resources into Jim.

The awkward silence apparent after this exchange was deafening. Linda, seeing an opportunity to change the topic and contribute, spoke up. "Matt, here's another idea. We should continue to update our intranet site as often as possible and consider putting together a "newsletter" for the organization on hot-button issues. Maybe you can add one of your famous cartoons each month. I know the entire organization loves your use of these during your presentations. This would be a proactive way to make sure all of our divisions know about any significant, and quite possibly, systemic issues."

Jim thought Linda's comments were ill-timed, and he was right, from *his* perspective. Matt reacted very differently. "That's a great idea, Linda! Did I hear you volunteer to spearhead this effort?" Linda hadn't exactly thought about it as *volunteering*, but since it was her idea, and she was excited by it, immediately retorted in a positive and firm voice: "Absolutely. I will start right away!" Matt knew he had put Linda on the spot, but he loved how she handled it.

The discussion continued for another 20 minutes, with both Linda and Meghan bringing up additional novel ideas and Jim remaining completely silent, not making much effort to listen. Dalton played observer, or facilitator, during the meeting, taking in the ideas, but not affecting the group's chemistry. After an hour, they broke for a quick coffee-break.

After the break, Dalton walked everyone through his shortlist of the key aspects of an effective Audit Outreach program, including building effective connections with employees, establishing relationships with management, and educating the organization. He began to discuss each point in detail with the team, with Matt's encouragement. Linda and Meghan had continued to add their ideas on the subject, while Jim remained silent, continuing to convey his disinterest in the whole project.

Dalton went on, "This is always an exciting issue for me to discuss, because I think promoting Audit effectively and establishing fruitful relationships are both extremely important for the ultimate success of an organization. To work with a team of this caliber, I am sure I will gain some new ideas that I can use moving forward as well. So, let's start from the top: building effective relationships within the organization. Some key aspects of Building Effective Relationships include: *transparency*, *building trust*, *active listening*, and *continuous communications*.

"Let's spend a few minutes on each. Transparency, in my opinion, is the key to an effective Internal Audit department. Matt has long been a proponent of this concept and I share his views. So, there is not much more to go through here. The MultiCrown Internal Audit department seems very transparent to me, which is displayed by:

▪ Publishing internally the annual audit risk assessment and audit plan.
▪ Walking auditees through the audit-level risk assessment to verify agreement and understanding.

- Sharing the categories of the audit work programs so that auditees clearly understand the audit scope.
- During the audit, communicating each issue or observation as soon as identified and working with auditees to determine how to best mitigate risks.

"You guys do all of these things, and I think it's a big part of your success. Now, because of your transparent approach, I believe that trust continues to build inside the organization." As Dalton spoke, Jim continued physically signaling his obvious disgust and disapproval. His body was turned away from Dalton, conveying disinterest and disagreement. He also continued to play with his smart phone while leaning back in his chair, not once looking up.

Meghan chimed in. "When I first started here, I have to admit, I thought you were a little crazy, Matt. Over the past months, however, I've seen the light. The trusting relationships that have been built by our audit team, I think, have been based on this approach." Matt nodded his head in appreciation. He was never very comfortable with direct compliments, but that didn't mean he did not like to hear them. Jim continued to bite his lip during the discussion of transparency, suppressing commentary. He still believed this began to border on an independence issue. He always believed in a strict separation, even a wall, between the organization and Audit.

Dalton continued, "Trust is built through not only transparency, but also numerous other aspects of relationship building. These include an active audit outreach program, which we covered earlier. Audit should reach out to management throughout the organization, at least quarterly, to gain management's pulse on risks and issues. These meetings begin to build trust through face-to-face interactions where Audit can show its value and listen to business concerns. The more you get to know people on a personal level, the more trust can be built. This is also a wonderful opportunity to show management that auditors can be much more than auditors. We can stay focused on risk, protecting the company, and on asking *positive* questions. What do I mean by 'positive' questions? One of the standard initial risk assessment questions is, 'What could go wrong?' Everyone uses it, but I think it's not a very good *initial* question. Why? It is inherently negative. It's like starting a conversation with anyone who has kids with, 'What's wrong with your kids?' instead of, 'How are your kids?' Bad way to start a conversation and a bad way to start a relationship. Now, what is a better, more positive question? How about we focus on the objectives of management? We can start with, 'What are your organization's goals and objectives?' This spurs conversation with the auditee and focuses on the positives of what they are doing at work. After this discussion, my follow-up question would be, 'What are the major issues or risks that might be hindering you from meeting your objectives?' Really, it's the same as asking them 'What could go wrong?' but in a much more positive manner. This way, it's clear that Audit is trying to help management meet its goals. Remember guys, it is not only *what* you say that's important—*how* you say it is also critical."

At this point, Matt realized Dalton had entered his "presenter mode." His suit jacket was off, cufflinks removed, and sleeves rolled up, and he began pacing around the conference room, increasingly utilizing broad gestures as he spoke. Matt could also tell that Dalton had done this little presentation more than a few times. It did not seem canned, but more of a well-known topic.

Dalton continued, "The next thing we need to discuss on promoting the audit function is effective communications, including Active Listening. Of course, this is a critical P-C skill for everything, not *just* for promoting Audit." Dalton continued to make eye contact with everyone in the room, to make sure everyone was engaged. Obviously, there was one consistent dissenter, whom Dalton ignored, albeit with difficulty. Everyone else had kept good eye contact; in fact, Dalton had to look away from Meghan as she stared back at him intently. It was a good thing that he knew that three-to-five seconds is about the maximum two people should hold each other's eye contact and "gaze" at each other; after that, it gets very awkward in front of others.

"Depending on what study is being quoted, we remember a dismal 25 to 50 percent of what we hear. Utilizing strong, active listening skills will also help maximize the effectiveness of relationship-building sessions. Active Listening is when the listener provides feedback, both verbal and nonverbal, to the speaker, demonstrating that the speaker's message has been understood. Active Listening tends to involve *communicating* verbally and nonverbally, *practicing* 'uninterrupted' listening, *restating* the message, and *observing* the sender's nonverbal signals. We should all practice Active Listening because it helps us understand others better, show others we respect them and the conversation, allows us to receive accurate messages, and enables us to respond appropriately."

In his daylong seminars, Dalton loved to discuss body language at the end of the day. This way, he could talk about what he had picked up during the day. He did somewhat embarrass some attendees a bit, but in a positive and nonconfrontational way. However, in this meeting, it didn't seem appropriate as each person's body language was screaming what they were thinking. Meghan was very engaged, leaning forward, smiling consistently, and nodding her head approvingly. Linda's body language, similar to Meghan's, but a little more laid back, also represented full engagement. She took copious notes and traded ideas with Meghan throughout the meeting. Jim, on the other hand, was very disengaged.

Matt noted all of this, not seemingly discouraged or upset at Jim. Matt began to add to the discussion with Dalton, actively moving around the room to see whose eyes would follow. All did, with one obvious exception. "I learned years ago the importance of nonverbal communication. Actually, my first date with my lovely wife was far from perfect. I had a bad day and, at dinner, she was definitely very engaging and I was enjoying myself. However, my vocal tone was low, and I was shy, so I did not hold eye contact well. She later told me that my shoulders were hunched. If my future wife hadn't looked past this and given me some time to adjust, I would not be the luckiest man alive today!" Matt exclaimed. Dalton had heard this story before and believed Matt told it for a very specific reason—to continue to observe Jim's negative reaction and see how Meghan and Linda would react. The results were predictable.

Dalton continued at the flipchart, scribbling madly as he talked:

Some Active Listening Techniques
- Using encouraging words and reassuring sounds to convey interest ("I see.").
- Restating in your own words what the person said ("To make sure I understood you correctly, I heard you say . . . is that correct?").
- Reflecting to show you understand how they feel ("You seemed pretty upset by this . . .").
- Probing the interviewee's initial response in order to expand and/or clarify the information given ("Please tell me more about that . . .").
- Summarizing ("These seem to be the main ideas you stated . . .").

Meghan took advantage of his pause. "Dalton, I see your point. So, eye contact is very important and restating in summary format is another technique. You seem very passionate about listening. . . ." Her voice began to trail off as she started to laugh, with Dalton, Linda, and Matt joining in. Meghan had done a great job of throwing everything Dalton was talking about right back at him. Dalton blushed slightly, which was very rare for him.

Dalton smiled in appreciation, but continued. "Meghan, as your *sarcasm* can attest, these Active Listening techniques can be used to show the speaker you are listening and understanding his point of view.

"Now, *Active* Listening is very helpful, but that is only a small facet of *effective* listening skills. Optimizing our listening skills can make us much stronger internal auditors. Here are 10 easy steps to optimize your listening." Dalton pulled out copies of a document from his computer bag and handed them out to everyone, although he had to wave the page at Jim a few times to catch his attention. He then proceeded to go through each point.

Optimizing Listening Skills

1. Avoid interruptions as much as possible, including calls or texts.
2. Try to adhere to the 70/30 rule. Aim to spend at least 70 percent of a conversation time listening and less than 30 percent talking.
3. Stay in the present; thinking about off-subject topics or your next question detracts from listening.
4. Reduce noise and distractions as much as possible.
5. Abstain from multitasking.
6. Look at the other person and focus on the words and meanings.
7. Resist jumping to conclusions.
8. Take on the responsibility of listening: being bored, not liking the speaker, or disagreeing with what he or she has to say does not excuse you from actively listening.
9. Consider body language and respond with both words and actions, taking into account your own body language and facial expressions.
10. Restate key points to ensure accuracy and prevent potential misunderstandings.

Matt had consistently worked to improve his listening skills since he met his wife many years ago. He had discovered, in the early years of his happy marriage, that good listening skills were invaluable in a relationship. So he chimed in, wanting to make sure the group understood the importance of what Dalton had just stated.

"I think Dalton has a great point here. I know this discussion of promoting Internal Audit seems to have turned into more of a P-C skill discussion, but isn't that really what an Outreach of Audit program really is? Making sure that we have the pulse of our clients, personalizing our relationships, and helping people understand that we really care? To me, these skills are one and the same. As an aside, I've also asked Dalton to videotape the team in certain situations so we can effectively understand our body language and gesture clusters."

The discussion of the Outreach plan went on for a few more hours. Meghan happily offered to draft a formal plan for Matt to review. Everyone could definitely see the more positive attitude Meghan was exhibiting, and it was clearly helping the team's overall productivity.

• • •

Three weeks later, Matt, Meghan, and Dalton flew to Mobile to meet with Karl Saint at the Plastic Molding Division headquarters. Karl had specifically asked Matt if Dalton could also join them as he'd heard about some of Dalton's work within the organization. Karl had some ideas he wanted to explore with Dalton. Dalton was very excited about the meeting with Karl. There seemed to be some additional opportunities beginning to percolate at MultiCrown through the highly regarded work Dalton had done, and with Matt's constant praise to his fellow executives. Dalton was also anticipating seeing the new and improved Meghan in action. Her "true" personality was coming out, and her sharp intelligence and craftsmanship were emerging. Matt concurred; he was starting to really believe that once he was able to transfer into operations in a few years, he might have his internal replacement ready. At dinner, the guys stayed in their traveling clothes; Matt in slacks and a polo shirt and Dalton in jeans and a pullover. Meghan, however, seemed to be ready for a bit more flash. She'd changed into a black skirt and top, and to Dalton, she looked stunning. Dinner didn't run late since they had an early morning meeting with Karl and had a flight back Chicago later in the afternoon.

• • •

Matt, Meghan, and Dalton arrived at the Mobile plant around 8:40 for their 9:00 A.M. meeting with Karl. Karl had made a few procedural changes in his first weeks, one mainly around the productivity of the office personnel. He instituted a new procedure to not have any meetings prior to 9 A.M. or after 4 P.M. The focus was to let employees have some time to get organized and get their own work completed and not have meeting paralysis, which was prevalent in this division. Walking into Karl's office right at 9 A.M., they were greeted by a tall, somewhat imposing man. Karl Saint stood at least 6'3" and had to be over 250 pounds. By no means heavy or in perfect shape, Karl seemed to have achieved the balance between the two. Karl was clean-shaven from his head to his face. With his light hair color, it was even hard to see his eyebrows. He was dressed in brown slacks, full cuff, with brown-and-white wingtips and a navy-blue-and-white hounds-tooth-patterned shirt. Just from his appearance and personal style, Dalton thought they were going to get along just fine.

Karl greeted the team with a hearty *hello* and went through the natural first-time meeting introductions. Matt and Dalton were always outgoing, but Meghan was making both of them look like amateurs with her dynamic, vivacious personality. Meghan appeared to have quickly discovered that her personality, intelligence, charm, and outgoing nature could help her get far in any organization. Matt was very impressed with her; it did appear that Dalton's outgoing persona was rubbing off on her.

After the introductions wound down and after a brief, spirited discussion of the Bowl Championship Series versus the pending College Football Playoff, the group got down to business, and Matt jumped into a short introduction.

"Karl, thank you so much for taking the time to meet with us. I know you are busy, but we believe that Internal Audit can assist you in many ways. Over the past few weeks, we revamped our Audit Outreach plan and I'm really excited about the things we will be doing to continue to communicate to the company how we can help. However, based on talking with you for just a few minutes and your initial actions during your limited tenure at MultiCrown, I can see that you *get it.* Instead of walking through the presentation, I would rather just discuss how we can help you and get a better understanding of what your goals, objectives, and needs are. Meghan, would you like to take Karl through this?" Matt knew that, rightly, *he* should be the one having this discussion with a new division president; however, he really wanted Meghan to develop her critical relationship-building skills, and there was nothing like real-life practice.

Meghan excitedly began, "Karl, again, thanks for your time. I know you have a significant undertaking on your hands, and I am sure it's very exciting. That's why we're here—we want to *help* you get this division where it should be and reach its potential." While speaking, Meghan gently leaned toward Karl but not to the point of being overbearing. Her legs were crossed tightly but pointing at Karl, which she knew to be an easy way of reassuring the person you are speaking with that you're speaking to them and only them. Dalton continued to be impressed. Meghan was following many of the body language concepts they had discussed. For Meghan to implement them so effectively, so quickly, was amazing. She seemed to be a natural at this.

Karl seemed equally impressed. "This conversation is refreshing. When I was at PetroChem, we went through a few Audit executives. When I left, a gentleman by the name of Steve Wesson was there and he enlightened me on how Audit can really help my organization. Steve and I became fast friends and we still keep in touch. In fact, that's one of the main reasons I wanted Dalton here today."

Dalton thought this might have been the reason, but had not been sure until now. Dalton smiled and nodded appreciatively at this comment. No need to say much; Dalton had worked with Steve prior to his joining PetroChem and they were longtime friends. In fact, Steve was one of Dalton's first recurring training clients and they had dinner any time Dalton was in San Diego. The consistent feedback Dalton always received was that he was very outgoing and truly caring. He made an effort to establish not only business relationships, but also friendships with his clients. This endorsement to Karl was indicative of his friendship with Steve.

Meghan continued, "That's great to hear; it's very refreshing to see a leader who really understands what Audit is about, and knows we can do more than stare at numbers and do taxes. Let's start at the top. People tend to forget that our goal as internal auditors is to help the organization achieve its objectives; in fact, it's right there in the formal definition of Internal Audit. That being said, let's talk about your division. What are your goals over the next year?"

Karl liked being around smart people; right now, he liked the situation very much. "Meghan, Matt, and Dalton, I'm here for a very specific reason: to turn around this underperforming division. In the few days I've been here, I've been a bit surprised to see how antiquated the systems are and quite frankly how creaky and inefficient the processes are. To me, it seems that both of these issues have contributed to the lackadaisical attitude prevalent here. We seem to have accepted our fate and acted as if we cannot change the path we are on. My goal is to refocus this division and improve its profit margin to be *over* the industry average. What I want to do is begin a legacy here that will continue long after I am gone. We're also focusing on development and enhancement of our current products, and also working to align our culture with the corporate culture of the rest of MultiCrown." As Matt heard this last point, he realized that Caleb must have specifically mentioned the need for culture realignment to Karl.

"I've been a bit surprised at the lack of energy around this division. I've seen employees being stagnated and accepting losing rather than taking that next step. I have also been worried about the looseness of the internal controls, and especially the fraud controls. I read your past audit reports of the units of this division, and I agree with what you recommended. I don't understand the resistance and defensiveness I read to your valid observations and recommendations. I further see a real lack of creativity, and observed serious issues with the organizational structure. . . . I am beginning to ramble. I do not believe we are being overly ambitious this year; we are setting up some realistic and sustainable goals for the future." Karl continued for the next 10 minutes discussing some specific goals for the group and what his plans were for the upcoming year. As Karl talked, Meghan had been asking probing questions to make sure she understood, and she continued to use the Active Listening skills Dalton had taught her. Karl seemed to really enjoy this intelligent line of discussion from Meghan.

During this conversation, Meghan was taking notes—complete, but not overly detailed, high-level bulleted notes. She focused on capturing the main themes and wrote down phrases to recall any follow-up questions she might have. Dalton looked over at Matt, communicating without words their appreciation for how good a job Meghan was doing. Both took some notes, and both wanted to jump into the conversation at times, but decided Meghan had things well under control.

After Karl finished explaining his objectives and priorities, Meghan said, "Karl, thank you very much for your comments. That was a very helpful overview. Based on your goals for the year, what I would like to do is shift the conversation and discuss the major hurdles you foresee in meeting your goals." Meghan asked about each goal, using what Dalton called *restating*, one of the many Active Listening techniques. As Karl discussed the major obstacles and possible risks, Meghan summarized some of the key obstacles and risks in her notes, including:

- Old computer systems; dialogue with Corporate as to how to upgrade them.
- Inconsistent and poorly executed processes. Improve, and eventually optimize processes going forward. Lean/Six Sigma review.
- Lack of understanding of production waste and how to reduce this waste.
- Reorganizing and reviewing staffing to get the right people into the right jobs to meet their aggressive goals.
- Upgrading the weak internal control structure, particularly giving initial priority to the fraud and operational controls.

After taking a short coffee-break, Meghan got right back to the key obstacles and risks. "Karl, this is very helpful. As you know, our goal is to be a trusted resource for management. That being said, I believe that in some of the areas you have mentioned, we could be of significant assistance, specifically in the systems review area, analyzing processes and helping upgrade the internal controls. I can feel Matt's glare on me right now, so, let me put a caveat on what I just said." Matt was looking at Meghan and, without knowing or being able to control it, his face reflected his concern. His eyebrows were raised ever so slightly and his eye twitched. But with Meghan's comment, his expressions turned into an understanding smile.

Meghan continued, "As we all know, we utilize a risk-based approach to auditing. Since we're midway through the year, our basic audit plan has been set for the year. However, I'm fortunate to work with a very progressive audit function. We are big proponents of what we call Continuous Risk Assessment. As part of my role in Internal Audit, I meet with our teams and continue to gather information on the organization, trends, new risks, and other issues that pop up. At least monthly, or as deemed necessary, the Audit management team gets together and takes a look at the current risk assessment and adjusts accordingly. Your division has been high on our risk assessment for the past few years for all of the reasons you mentioned. That being said, I believe we can reassess our audit coverage and shift the resources necessary from regular audit engagements to consultative-type projects to assist you as soon as possible."

Again, both Dalton and Matt were very happy they had not jumped into the conversation. Meghan had done a fantastic job in establishing a very positive business relationship with Karl and properly promoting the services of the Audit group. Matt knew that a good leader needs to give his key employees opportunities to be successful and to learn, and he was glad he had given Meghan this opportunity to grow and shine.

Karl smiled broadly. "Meghan, this is *exactly* what I was looking for. What I want to do now is set the baseline for where things are today and identify possible improvements. You folks can help me greatly with this. My staff is overloaded, and quite frankly, they don't have the skills your team has, and I *really* need a fresh and independent point of view."

"Dalton, based on what we've discussed, I'm sure you can see the need for some training for my team. I would like you to put together a potential training program to start in the next few months, not only for my management team, but also for specific areas of our business. I don't want a lack of communication and teamwork to hinder our success."

Dalton's excitement was obvious; the ultimate compliment for a trainer is a referral. "Karl, I'd love to, but I want to make sure we balance this with the additional areas Matt and I have discussed for his team." As a small organization, Dalton could be very successful with a few large clients utilizing him throughout the year. But obtaining several new multibillion-dollar clients would take his business from one trainer to the delicate issue of scalability and hiring other trainers.

Karl immediately replied, "Sure, I understand you already have obligations, we just need to work into your schedule."

Matt asked Dalton and Meghan for a moment of private discussion with Karl so he could discuss some the concerns about the remaining leaders in the division and the poor state of the controls. While Matt was sure Caleb would discuss this with Karl at the right time, he wanted to give him his own observations as well. It was really important to establish a close collaborative relationship with Karl, and this was a good opportunity to begin.

Leaving Karl's office, Dalton was about to reaffirm Meghan's performance but, based on her body language, this was unnecessary. Her demeanor indicated she was ecstatic with how the meeting had gone. She was smiling broadly, and showed increased arm movement, and walked with extreme confidence to the break room. As soon as they entered the break room, Dalton was a bit surprised by a very warm hug and kiss from Meghan. Dalton, never bashful, blushed at this since it was no normal co-worker hug; it was deep, warm, and the kiss lingered, not that Dalton minded one bit. However, for both of their sakes, Dalton was glad they were alone in the break room.

"Dalton, I just wanted to thank you for all your help! I think it really paid off today. When we get back to town, I would love to take you to dinner to show my appreciation." Dalton replied, "Meghan, I only coached you and gave you advice; I deserve no credit—you deserve it all. Fantastic performance! Dinner isn't necessary but I would love to see you, regardless." Meghan blushed at this last comment and lightly brushed Dalton's shoulder. Matt found them a few minutes later and they headed to the airport.

● ● ●

They boarded the MD-80 flight to Chicago O'Hare Airport, all upgraded to first class once again. On the way to the airport, with the exception of getting stuck in traffic on Airport Parkway, the feelings and comments were all positive, and there wasn't much of a need to debrief. Matt praised Meghan for her handling of the meeting and had nothing but very complimentary things to say. He was very excited about assisting Karl and was now thinking through how to juggle his audit calendar to make these additional assignments work. Meghan was beaming, and Dalton was very excited about the continued opportunities with Karl moving forward. He also hoped that the professional relationship and friendship with Meghan would continue to blossom into a romantic one. He also definitely owed Steve an email and dinner for the referral and would ask Matt to join them if they could all get to the same city at the same time.

Dalton spent the flight to Chicago working on his laptop, honing the body-language course he was developing. He planned to discuss this in more detail with Matt during the flight. This new course was getting very strong interest from his clients. They were learning that body language has its own vocabulary and way of speaking. People communicate nonverbally with the help of different cues or signals that are grouped together or strung together in a sequence, usually within three to five seconds of the initial gesture being made. It's very similar to the way different words create a meaningful sentence. One word may not convey the message, but a complete sentence easily makes sense.

The total combination of different sensory stimuli, facial expressions, gestures, movements, postures and paralinguistic clues convey a distinct message. Many people make the mistake of trying to interpret each gesture in isolation, often leading to complete misunderstanding. Like composing sentences, the gestures need to be put together, in something called clustering. A cluster makes more sense out of a distinct nonverbal message.

Dalton thought about the previous group meeting with Jim. He had had his arms crossed over his chest, a self-defensive or controlling action. Jim was covering the vulnerable parts of his upper body. As Dalton recalled, it was definitely not a welcoming or open posture. But arms crossed aren't just a clue to being defensive when used in different clusters. Dalton recalled Jim's eyebrows scrunching, his neck postured downwards, and his total lack of eye contact.

The situation also played into Jim's physical reaction. It was already contentious and not cold in the room, so the fact that his arms were crossed, in addition to other gestures noted, indicated his emotional state.

While sitting next to each other on the plane, and discussing this during the flight, Dalton and Matt decided a course on body language was definitely a good idea for the team and the perfect time would be their semiannual team meeting before the holiday party in early December.

Dalton spent the rest of the flight developing an outline for the course he would give Matt's team. He wanted to move forward with this immediately, while it was fresh in his mind. Dalton knew the team would have a very full agenda based on Matt's preliminary suggestions; he wanted to give everyone a good overview of body language without digging too deeply, so he focused on the five most common gesture clusters: *defensiveness*, *evaluation*, *nervousness*, *impatience*, and *enthusiasm*.

As he went deep in thought about body language, he tuned out the world. Even his Scotch-on-the-rocks sat unattended as the ice melted. Dalton knew most people were unaware how often their physicality reveals what they are thinking or about to say. For example, Dalton recalled the many classic signs of defensiveness Jim had shown. He almost wished Jim's posture in the meeting was part of the videotaping Matt had requested; it would have been a perfect example. Other signs of defensiveness include a very rigid posture, tightly crossed arms or legs—almost appearing to be strained—difficulty looking the other party in the eyes, and fist clenching. As these words came to mind, he automatically typed them into a PowerPoint presentation. He knew he would need to organize and edit them later, but writing his thoughts as they came was his proven style for designing a new course.

When people are evaluating a situation or comment, they tend to tilt their head, a very common, subconscious gesture, possibly rubbing their cheek or chin and leaning forward—all of these showing interest. On the other hand, many people appear very nervous without knowing or understanding what their nonverbal signs or paralinguistic cues are showing. Like poker, we all have a "tell" or nervous tick. Dalton, through years of honing, had learned not to reveal his tick (it was squinting his eyes and repositioning his body). Every time he thought he might revert back, he would bite his lip or pinch his leg to remind himself how destructive these mannerisms could be—at least destructive to his poker winnings! His control over his tell had proven to be very effective.

Nervous indicators include constantly clearing their throat or twirling jewelry, tapping fingers, or any general fidgeting. Dalton recalled a situation when he interviewed a very qualified young man a few years back for a senior auditor position. The kid looked great on paper, but throughout the interview he couldn't stop his lip from twitching. He was very nervous, and it showed to somebody like Dalton, who paid attention to this. It was the main reason why he wasn't hired. If he was going to be that nervous in the interview, what was going to happen when he went out to meet with auditees—especially ones who pushed back aggressively?

The gesture cluster for impatience is easily confused with nervousness as they are very similar in many people. Impatience is indicated by the constant drumming of fingers, constant body movement, shifting in chair, foot swinging, and continuing to look at one's watch, the clock on the wall, or the door.

Dalton loved discussing the enthusiasm gesture cluster, as it was one that was pretty obvious to most, and one that he constantly projected. It was part of who he was. This attribute was one of the reasons he succeeded so well at training. His enthusiasm kept people paying attention and was contagious. Smiling, expressing numerous open hand gestures, with very open posturing, hands and arms open, body facing the other person instead of off to the side, wide eyes, and a lively voice were strong indicators of enthusiasm. Now he just hoped he was not appearing *too* enthusiastic when Meghan was around. He didn't want to be perceived as *needy*. As he thought about the people on Matt's staff, he thought Linda was the one who constantly displayed the enthusiasm gesture cluster.

People-Centric Skills Highlighted in This Chapter

Relationship Building

Building strong relationships is key to becoming an effective auditor. By building strong relationships, auditors build trust and the innate fear of auditors diminishes. Some habits of effective relationship builders include:

1. **Trust.** Trusting relationships start with transparency and open communication.
2. **It's okay to apologize.** Apologizing humanizes you and shows you are not perfect.
3. **Help before it's necessary.** It's easy to help when asked; auditors should volunteer assistance and continue to further understand the business risk profile so they can lend a hand without asking.
4. **Take responsibility.** Own your tasks, meet deadlines, and communicate when there are issues.
5. **Take an interest.** Exchange small-talk and take an interest in others. What is important to them needs to be important to you.
6. **Remember and recall.** Remembering someone's name or kids' ages or occupation, anything that shows, when you first met, that you remember them and the conversation. This will spark interest and solidify the relationship.

Optimized Listening Skills

Listening is one of the most important skills you can have. How well you listen has a major impact on your job effectiveness, and on the quality of your relationships with others. In fact, most of us are not good listeners, and research suggests that we remember only 25 to 50 percent of what we hear. That means that when you talk to your boss, colleagues, kids, or spouse, they'll recall less than half of the conversation.

By becoming a better listener, you can improve your productivity as well as your ability to influence, persuade, and negotiate. Following are 10 easy steps to optimize listening:

1. Avoid interruptions as much as possible, including calls or texts.
2. Try to adhere to the 70/30 rule. Aim to spend at least 70 percent of conversation time listening and less than 30 percent talking.

3. Stay in the present; thinking about off-subject topics or your next question detracts from listening.

4. Reduce noise and distractions as much as possible.

5. Abstain from multitasking.

6. Look at the other person and focus on the words and meanings.

7. Resist jumping to conclusions.

8. Take on the responsibility of listening. Being bored, not liking the speaker, or disagreeing with what he or she has to say does not excuse you from actively listening.

9. Consider body language and respond with both words and actions, taking into account your own body language and facial expressions.

10. Restate key points to ensure accuracy and prevent potential misunderstandings.

Active Listening

Active listening is a way of listening and responding to another person that improves mutual understanding. Active listening is a structured form of listening and responding that focuses the attention on the speaker. The listener must take care to attend to the speaker fully, and then repeat, in the listener's own words, what he or she thinks the speaker has said. The listener does not have to agree with the speaker—he or she must simply state what they think the speaker said.

Active listening tends to involve *communicating* verbally and non-verbally, *practicing* uninterrupted listening, *restating* the message, and *observing* the sender's nonverbal signals. We should all practice active listening because it helps us understand others better and show others we respect them and the conversation, allows us to receive accurate messages, and enables us to respond appropriately.

Some active listening techniques include:

- Using encouraging words and reassuring sounds to convey interest ("I see").
- Restating in your own words what the person said.
- Reflecting to show you understand how they feel ("You seemed pretty upset by this . . .").
- Probing the interviewee's initial response in order to expand and/or clarify the information given ("Please tell me more about that").
- Summarizing ("These seem to be the main ideas you stated").

(continued)

These active listening techniques can be used to show the speaker that you are listening and understanding his or her point of view.

Building Trust

An organization must trust the Internal Audit team to gain the most value from this department. Without trust, the proverbial doors are not open for Internal Audit to be successful. Additionally, the organization will not view Internal Audit as a trusted confidant and share significant or confidential information with Audit. Trust is built on the following four pillars:

- **Transparency.** If people believe you are hiding something, you will not be trusted. Be as transparent as possible in work relationships. As auditors, try not to hide what success looks like. If we are auditing based on a department's policies, and our audit work program is created based on the policy, why not share it with the auditee? They can gain an understanding of how we test by showing how and why we audit, not just *what* we are going to audit.
- **Continuous communication.** Make sure everyone knows exactly what you are doing and how you are doing it. One of the worst things to hear is, "I did not know" or "No one told me." Do not let anyone use that excuse; use clear communication and follow up.
- **Providing and accepting feedback.** As auditors, we want the auditee to own the audit and the results as much as possible. Ask for feedback as to how to make the audit better and more effective. Give feedback as well; be positive, but people appreciate honest feedback.
- **Walking the talk.** In order to build trust, Internal Audit must be aligned with the organization's goals and objectives. When necessary, admit mistakes but project the right message when speaking to clients that Audit can be a trusted advisor and meet any obligations they have committed to.

Body Language and Gesture Clusters

Body language is a form of nonverbal communication, where a person reveals clues to unspoken messages through physical behavior. Gesture clusters are when body language is interpreted by observing a group of movements and actions that reinforce a common message.

Gesture Clusters

- Defensiveness
  - Arms or legs crossed tightly
  - Scrunched/downward-directed eyebrows
  - Shoulders slumped
  - Downward posture
  - Absence of, or minimal, eye contact
  - Rigid posture
  - Fist clenching
- Evaluation
  - Tilting head sideways
  - Rubbing cheek or chin
  - Leaning forward
- Nervousness
  - Personal nervous tick (lips/eyes that twitch, foot tapping/swinging, etc.)
  - Clearing throat
  - Touching/playing with jewelry/watch
  - Tapping fingers
- Impatience
  - Drumming of fingers
  - Constant body movement
  - Continuing to check watch/clock
  - Turning body to closest exit
  - Continuing to glance at closest exit
- Enthusiasm
  - Smiling broadly
  - Open hand/body gestures
  - Wide eyes
  - Strong voice inflection

CHAPTER EIGHT

Continuing the
People-Centric Journey

M ATT WAS IN no hurry to make the 6:30 evening reservation at the premier steakhouse in Chicago. Matt, always on time for everything, knew Dalton would be a bit late. It was a blustery evening, with the winds gusting off Lake Michigan. Matt and Leslie, his wife, were invited for the evening by Dalton. Matt, the "Ethical Compass," as Dalton liked to think of him, might not have accepted an extravagant dinner from a consultant, if this was deemed "business." However, Dalton invited them for the holidays and just a few friends getting together, because that's what it really was. Dalton and Matt had become close over the past year and it felt, to both of them, like genuine friendship. Dalton had been over to Matt's house many times over the past year, from dinner to watching the Northwestern or Bears football games, and even having Matt's lovely wife watching Dalton's kids for a few hours.

Dalton in fact was at the restaurant a good 30 minutes early. He had plenty to think about. His business was growing explosively. With his first book out through a major publisher early next year, the sky was the limit. His business had more than doubled last year, and he had hired his first full-time employees. Dalton now saw his future clearly and was loving every minute of the journey. It wasn't just the monetary gains; it was the flexibility and ability to control his destiny. But it also was very much the mental and emotional high of speaking in front of a group and truly helping people. He had found his voice, and he was now speaking loud and clear.

As Matt and Leslie walked into the restaurant, exactly on time, Matt was taken aback to see Dalton already there, sitting patiently, slowly twirling a straw in what appeared to be a vodka-on-the-rocks. Dalton greeted both of his guests with his usual personal warmth. After a couple of cocktails, they played catchup, each updating the other with the occurrences of the past two months. The dinner ran long, friends catching up and reminiscing on the great year they had spent together.

Even after a couple of drinks, Matt remained composed and keenly aware of his facial expressions—especially in front of Dalton, with his highly developed people-reading skills. This was exactly why Dalton wanted to surprise Matt with his next question. "Matt, I gotta ask: Did you put Jim on MultiCrown's Performance Improvement Plan, or did you go ahead and cut him loose?" Dalton utilized these emotional words to see if he could elicit an interesting reaction. Matt smiled slightly, knowing full well what Dalton was attempting to do.

"Jim and I spoke back in early November; the tension was becoming obvious to everyone on the team. Jim is a bright guy, but not an ideal fit for us in Audit, so we had been looking for a position in IT for him. Last week, he received an offer to join the Infrastructure Team as a Technical Director. In that role, he will not have to work with people much, which he finally admitted was for the best. We were both very eager to move on." Matt drifted off on his comments about Jim, apparently not wanting to ruin the warm feelings of the fine evening.

The pre-dinner conversation continued as they slowly enjoyed their drinks, with all of them discussing the status of the Audit team members. It was obvious that Matt frequently discussed his people with Leslie, because she was nodding as Matt talked, and occasionally added an insightful comment. She often visited Matt to grab lunch, and she always made a point of talking with the auditors who were in the office. Matt suspected they liked Leslie a lot more than they liked him.

The tuxedoed waiter approached to get their order, interrupting their conversation. Dalton asked for his favorite, rare prime rib. Matt, as usual, requested the most unusual dish on the menu, and ordered caribou carpaccio. The thought of eating pounded raw caribou meat made Dalton shudder visibly, but this was now an old game for them, and Matt smiled at Dalton's grimace. Leslie, after carefully weighing her options, ordered the bouillabaisse, that flavorful and hearty French thick soup with clams, fish, scallops, and mussels.

Matt almost changed his mind to order the same thing, but ultimately they decided to share both dishes, a common practice for them.

With the waiter gone, Matt went on without skipping a beat in their line of discussion. "Linda has continued to advance very well and is positioned to succeed Jim sometime in the coming year. I promoted her to Senior Manager and I signed her up for the management training program at MultiCrown. We are also working on honing her leadership and presentation skills. The R&M team she's been leading is nearing its final test audits, and I think it will really pay off for MultiCrown. The R&M organization loves Linda, and I think if they could, would steal her away.

"Bill, after his learning experience with the difficult Tom, grew further into his managerial role and is steadily advancing and taking on increased responsibilities. I think in a couple of years he might be ready to move into the Financial/Operational Audit Director role. It's great to have capable people in the succession pipeline.

"Meghan has continued to really develop and blossom with her leadership responsibilities as Audit Director. She's widely seen as a rising star at Multi-Crown, and is also now a part of our advanced management training program. She's become close friends with Linda, and their mentoring relationship has been very helpful to both, in different ways. If I'm fortunate enough to be chosen to lead a division in a few years, she should be able to move into the Chief Audit Executive role."

Dalton did not need much of an update on Meghan. Their friendship and romantic relationship had continued to deepen. He had heard Meghan's perspective on how she was doing, but was glad that Matt wholeheartedly concurred. Matt and Leslie knew that Dalton and Meghan were getting more serious about each other, and Leslie chimed in, "Dalton, you better hang onto that one—she is a real catch!" To this comment from Leslie, Dalton smiled expansively. He was pleased, but also worried. After his recent divorce, he was a bit gun-shy.

"I'm not sure if you and Lila are still in close contact," Matt said cautiously. "She does not tell me much about her social life, but I think she is dating an architect. At least she introduced me to one when I bumped into them coming out of a fancy restaurant; both dressed in evening wear and heading to the symphony."

Dalton smiled in appreciation of Matt's careful tone. "We're still good friends and I have met her architect friend. We double-dated last week. They seem to be really great with each other. I really like Lila, but we both realized I can't be with a woman who reads my mind. Once, she got angry at what I was *thinking!*" At this comment, Matt shook his head in rueful understanding, but Leslie seemed a bit puzzled. Matt looked over at her and it was mutually understood that he would explain this later.

"You probably have not picked this up yet since I just had a discussion with Sandra yesterday," Matt said. "The president of the South America region wants to promote her to regional controller. Sandra was worried I might feel she is abandoning us. However, I told her it was a great opportunity, and given her long-term career goal of becoming our CFO, a fantastic step for her. She decided to accept the offer, and I'm sure she'll share this exciting news with you when you see her. Act surprised!"

Matt finished discussing his team, put down his glass of merlot, and looked Dalton straight in the eye. "Dalton, I believe when getting together with good friends, we both should leave enriched. I always feel that way with you, and I hope you feel the same. That being said, I wanted to sincerely thank you for all your efforts to improve my team this year. This is hands-down the best investment I've made in my people and you deserve all of the accolades you've received. In fact, expect calls from Royal Soda, PaperNote, Mountain Construction, and Mason's sometime after the holidays. At last week's Chief Audit Executive Roundtable, I told them what you had done for us, and I think they're all interested in using you next year. You may need to clone yourself, although the thought of more Daltons running around is really scary!" At this, all three laughed.

Dalton became very introspective for a few moments, and Matt and Leslie knew to give him a little space. His year had been full of seismic changes. Businesswise, the year had been extremely successful. He had started to field initial inquiries to sell his company and partner with one of the largest audit training organizations in the country. On the other hand, his divorce took a significant toll on him emotionally. He felt like he would never get married again; but now, maybe that was changing. And his kids—they were everything to him. In fact, after the MultiCrown training this week, he was taking the kids and Meghan on a very well-deserved 14-day cruise throughout the Mediterranean. All of this fed into his reaction to Matt's wonderful compliments. He choked up, and a tear threatened to fall from his eye. "Matt, I'm not sure you'll ever understand how much that means to me. I pour my heart and soul into every client. The only way I become successful is through strong relationships and referrals. Nothing much else to say about that except *thank you.*" Dalton went on to discuss his continued role with MultiCrown. Karl Saint, the new head of the Plastic Moldings Division, had engaged him to develop his team. To top it off, Caleb's discussion of Dalton's work with the Audit Committee opened the door to further opportunities.

They all toasted to the wonderful year that was quickly concluding and continued the discussion on the upcoming training week that Dalton was assisting with. Dalton was a bit apprehensive to see Meghan, Lila, and Sandra *all* at the same time. What if they started to compare notes? However, with Leslie present, he did not want to mention this at all.

Dalton thoughtfully paid the tab, over Matt's pro-forma objections, and, after a very convivial evening, they headed their separate ways.

· · ·

On Friday morning, Dalton sat in the back of Training Room 1A and caught up with many of the team members before the morning's training began. The team had convened all week on a variety of subjects, culminating with today's People-Centric discussions. Dalton was only scheduled to speak for a total of 10 hours throughout the week but, with Matt's blessings, wanted to spend time with the team to see how they were developing. He had really enjoyed the week and could see that the morale of the team was very high. Everyone seemed to enjoy this week of wrap-up, training, and planning meetings, culminating with the Audit Holiday Party on Saturday night. The event always included the auditors' spouses or dates. As usual, Matt hadn't told anyone what the plan was; it was always a surprise. And almost every year, it was a *great* surprise. Last year was a murder mystery dinner; the year before was a suite at the Bulls game; the year before that was a laser-tag game for the entire team, including children, followed by a casual dinner at a neighborhood Italian restaurant. Dalton was very pleased that Matt had invited him to join the team for their holiday gathering this year.

Matt kicked off the day with a summary of the department progress for the year and key initiatives for next year. They had worked on that in much more detail the day before, but he wanted to make sure the goals were really understood.

Meghan and Linda were up next, discussing presentation and interviewing skills and the upcoming competency assessments for next year. Per Matt's request, Linda and Meghan also teamed up to give a detailed description of the teaming challenges and lessons of the R&M/Audit team. They all laughed as Linda described how bewildered the three engineers were when they first met Dalton, following what had become known as the Chicken Truck Wreck Lateness Excuse.

Again, at Matt's suggestion, Bill presented a session on conflict management, describing his experience with Tom Peterson. He recalled how worried he'd been when they flew to Mobile to confront Tom, with Matt putting him on point. He said this in a way to make everyone smile in commiseration. Many of them had faced Tom Peterson in the past.

Matt gave a very well-received presentation on assessing corporate cultures and subcultures. It was obvious that Matt had a deep interest in *cultural anthropology*, and his enthusiasm for the topic was infectious. This led to an hour of lively discussion on the various subcultures of MultiCrown.

Dalton then teamed up with Meghan to review building effective business relationships using her comments and observations of their meeting with Karl, as he'd come on board as the new president of the Plastics Molding Division. Finally, last on the agenda, Dalton started on listening skills and body language.

The week ended with a little treat Dalton put together for the team. Matt had given Dalton videos of the team in public-speaking sessions from last year's Toastmasters daylong session on public speaking. He then played very recent videos of the staff conducting mock interviews. They went through each staff member's before-and-after videos. The team had a high level of comfort with each other that made the analysis educational, but also fun for all. Freezing selected scenes or putting them in slow motion with the DVD controls, and using a laser pointer, Dalton highlighted the nonverbal expressions and behavior clusters. The team loved this activity, and they all laughed good-naturedly at the foolish-looking frozen expressions. One of the highlights was the team counting the number of *umm*'s and *ahh*'s Ivan Leong, the Audit Manager from the Singapore Audit Office, said in the span of a four-minute speaking session (the count was over 50!). Ivan took this in good spirit, as when they viewed his "after" video, he was very smooth and crisp, and the count was down to 2 in total. When the staff good-naturedly applauded this great progress, Ivan stood and gave courtly bow. This led to a new round of laughter.

Dalton was really excited about this new nonverbal communications course, as he had received significant interest in analyzing body language, in addition to running personality assessments for teams, and team-building courses based on the assessments.

As the day drew to a close, Matt slowly sipped his robust coffee, slightly squinting his eyes in pleasure after each strong gulp. Watching the team, he felt like a proud parent. Being able to develop the auditors in such a positive manner was one of the things he enjoyed most about his work.

Matt looked over to find Dalton staring into space, and interrupting his reverie, said, "It's been a great week, my friend; thanks for everything. I hope you're joining us for dinner tomorrow night; it will really be a fun night for everyone!" Dalton snapped out of his introspective moment. "Matt, you're very welcome and I wouldn't miss dinner for the world. But *tell* me, what is the surprise this year?"

"Well, Dalton, it *is* a surprise, but since it's *you* asking, and everybody will know in a few minutes anyway, I can tell you we are doing a dinner cruise on Lake Michigan!" Matt noted the pleased and approving smile on Dalton's face. He then stood up to address the full team prior to breaking up a bit early this Friday afternoon.

"I want to take this opportunity to again talk about our People-Centric journey. I call it a *journey*, because even with all we have learned over the past year, we have much more to learn, and in fact we should all work on improving these skills our entire careers. I know, even with my *many* years of work experience, *I'm* still striving to improve these skills. As I have said many times, having great technical skills gets you through the door, but to really succeed as an auditor, and as a businessperson, you *also* need to master communication and interpersonal skills. With Dalton's help, we have worked on learning how to manage conflicts, launching and leading teams, reaching consensus, brainstorming ideas, avoiding groupthink, coaching and mentoring employees, improving our listening skills, establishing positive relationships, promoting the audit function, beginning to understand nonverbal communications and body language, and assessing corporate cultures and subcultures. I'm personally looking forward to continuing on this journey of learning and development."

Matt took a deep breath, and went on, "Everyone—great week! Thank you for your participation and attention; this was probably the best training and planning week we have ever had. Our surprise this year is a dinner cruise on Lake Michigan. We are leaving from Navy Pier at 6:30, in time for drinks at sunset!" At this news the staff erupted in cheers and applause.

Matt was not finished, but paused for effect. "One more thing: As everyone knows, Dalton has been a big part of our success this past year. Due to his assistance, I think our team has grown tremendously. We will definitely find other projects for him next year with new training initiatives. For example, since we are a global company, we really need to understand how our People-Centric skills must adjust when we are interacting in different cultures. We also need to go through a session where we can assess our own personalities and learn how to work effectively with people with *other* types of personalities. Also, we could use a session on how to work with difficult people. I'm sure you all have had to deal with a few of those!" He said this so drily, the auditors chuckled. "Also, there is the entire subject of Emotional Intelligence that is in essence *advanced* People-Centric skills."

Matt continued: "I did want to present Dalton with a MultiCrown polo shirt and personalized portfolio as a very small token of appreciation for his efforts with us this year. Of course, these are in addition to the *modest* consulting fees he charged us. Also, by the powers vested in me, Dalton is henceforth an honorary member of the MultiCrown Audit team, with full powers to *annoy* anybody!" Matt's summation and Dalton's efforts were met with a rousing ovation.

Dalton, not one to easily embarrass, was thoroughly and obviously overwhelmed by Matt's gesture and compliments. "Everyone, I can't thank you enough for inviting me into your shop and accepting me as one of your own. As clients, you're everything I could ever ask for!" Dalton said this while speaking to the entire team but his gaze turned to Meghan and stopped there for a moment.

Matt then turned to the entire group. "Enjoy this evening, and we'll see everyone at dinner tomorrow!"

With this last comment, the team headed out to enjoy happy hour for a rousing end to a great week of training. Many clustered around Dalton on the way out to make sure he was joining them for the dinner cruise on the following day. Dalton and Matt smiled in mutual satisfaction and wordlessly walked out side by side.

About the Authors

Danny M. Goldberg is the founder of GOLDSRD (www.GOLDSRD.com), a leading provider of Staff Augmentation, Executive Recruiting, and Professional Development services. Previously, Danny led the Professional Development and Executive Recruiting Practices at Sunera. Mr. Goldberg re-purchased his practice that he sold to Sunera in 2011. Prior to joining Sunera in January 2011, Danny founded SOFT GRC, an advisory services and professional development firm. Danny has over 16 years of audit experience, including five as a CAE/audit director at two diverse companies. The Professional Development Practice at GOLDSRD has *over 100 full-day courses* available for clients that can be customized. These courses include topical matters on Internal Audit, Audit, Finance, and People-Centric (Soft Skills).

Prior to founding SOFT GRC, Danny was the director of SOX Compliance and Corporate Audit at Dr. Pepper Snapple Group, where he led the Year One SOX Compliance efforts and assisted in building both departments. Prior to his tenure at Dr. Pepper, Danny was Chief Audit Executive at Tyler Technologies, a publicly traded technology company (Danny was hired to build the department from the ground up).

Danny has served on the audit committee of the Dallas Independent School District and was the chairman of the North Texas Leadership Council of the American Lung Association in 2012. Danny is also the IIA Dallas and Fort Worth Chapter Programs Committee co-chairman for the 2012–2013 year and was elected to the Fort Worth IIA Board of Directors in 2013. Danny has also been asked to serve on the IIA's Learning Committee for the 2014–2016 term.

Danny is accredited as the professional commentator on the publication *BNA Tax and Accounting Portfolio, Internal Auditing: Fundamental Principles* (Accounting Policy and Practice Series), which is authored by renowned audit scholars Curtis C. Verschoor and Mort A. Dittenhofer—co-author of *Sawyer's Internal Auditing*. Additionally, Danny has been named as one of the Fort Worth Business Press 40 Under 40 for 2014.

He has also published numerous articles in trade magazines, including:

- College and University Auditor ("Project Management: Crucial Skills for Internal Auditors," Winter 2014, Featured Article)
- *The Audit Report* ("Critical Thoughts on Critical Thinking," June 2013, cover article)
- *ISACA Journal* ("The Importance of the ARA," Volume 4, 2012)
- *ISACA Journal* ("The Missing Piece: Optimized Interpersonal Skills," Volume 3, 2012)
- *The Audit Report* ("Executive Search: Knowing the Company Is as Important as Knowing the Candidate," December 2011)
- *ISACA Journal* ("General Auditing for the IT Auditor: An Overview," Volume 3, 2011)
- *The Audit Report* ("11 Hot Topics for 2011," March 2011)
- *Dallas Business Journal* ("The Yes-Man Phenomenon," January 2011)

Danny is a well-known speaker across the nation at numerous IIA- and ISACA-sponsored events. He currently works with over 100 professional associations around the world and numerous Fortune 1000 companies, assisting in their professional development efforts.

Danny is a Certified Public Accountant, Certified Internal Auditor, and Certified Information Systems Auditor, is certified in the Governance of Enterprise Information Technology, certified in Risk and Information Systems Control, and certified in Risk Management Assurance, has obtained his certification in Control Self-Assessment, and is a Chartered Global Management Accountant.

Manny Rosenfeld has had the privilege of serving four Fortune 500 industrial companies and a leading global financial services organization during his 34-year career. He has had the Chief Audit Executive role for the past 14 years.

Manny currently works for MoneyGram International as Senior Vice President of Internal Audit. MoneyGram is the world's second-largest money transfer and payment company, with 340,000 agents in 200 countries. Prior to MoneyGram, Manny worked for Commercial Metals Company (CMC) as Vice President of Audit. CMC is a global, vertically integrated metals company. Before that, he was Vice President of Internal Audit for both TRW Automotive and Navistar Corporation, two global and diversified automotive companies. During his prior 20 years, while with Alcoa, he had a series of roles, including: Senior Audit Manager, Quality and Process Improvement Internal Consultant, Manager of Capital and Acquisitions Programs, Audit Supervisor, and Management Sciences/Industrial Engineering Consultant. Manny has led audit functions with satellite offices based in the United States, Spain, Brazil, Great Britain, Italy, and China.

He serves on the Board of Governors of the Dallas Chapter of the Institute of Internal Auditors, where he leads the Chief Audit Executive programs. Manny is a Certified Internal Auditor and has a certification in Risk Management Assurance. He also achieved a Lean/Six Sigma Black-Belt designation.

Manny graduated from Cornell University, where he earned a Master of Engineering in Management Sciences, a Master of Business Administration, and a Bachelor of Science in Industrial Engineering.

Both Manny and his wife of 32 years, Louise, share a love of cooking international foods and of going to interesting restaurants. Manny also enjoys reading science fiction, mysteries, military history, and most branches of science. He has traveled extensively throughout the world and speaks fluent Spanish. Manny has a regular fitness routine that he views as a required adjunct to a cooking hobby.